HAUNTED
CHESTERFIELD

HAUNTED CHESTERFIELD

CAROL BRINDLE

Frontispiece: *The crooked spire of Chesterfield parish church.*

First published in 2006 by Tempus Publishing

Reprinted in 2011 by
The History Press
The Mill, Brimscombe Port,
Stroud, Gloucestershire, GL5 2QG
www.thehistorypress.co.uk

© Carol Brindle 2011

The right of Carol Brindle to be identified as the Author
of this work has been asserted in accordance with the
Copyrights, Designs and Patents Act 1988.

All rights reserved. No part of this book may be reprinted
or reproduced or utilised in any form or by any electronic,
mechanical or other means, now known or hereafter invented,
including photocopying and recording, or in any information
storage or retrieval system, without the permission in writing
from the Publishers.

British Library Cataloguing in Publication Data.
A catalogue record for this book is available from the British Library.

ISBN 978 0 7524 4081 1

Typesetting and origination by Tempus Publishing Limited.
Printed in Great Britain.

CONTENTS

Acknowledgements		6
Introduction		7
1	Churches and Chapels	9
2	Hospitals	28
3	Houses Great and Small	35
4	Places of Business	49
5	Shops Now and Then	55
6	Theatres and Cinemas	60
7	Four Grand Halls and a Castle	65
8	Public Houses	79
Bibliography		95

ACKNOWLEDGEMENTS

I would like to thank the following people who have been of help to me. First and foremost all the people who have come on the ghost walk over the years, or listened to my ghost talk, and shared their experiences with me; Bernadette Wainwright, Tourism Officer for Chesterfield who first asked me to lead the ghost walks; Anne Krawszik, and other members of staff in the Local Studies section of the Chesterfield Library; Kathy Hollyer, chief executive of the Ashgate Hospice, for allowing me to tour the buildings, take photographs and talk to the staff; Jane Bridge, Head of Support Services, for taking a great deal of time to show me round, point out photograph opportunities and introduce me to the staff; Peter Hill, the owner of Bank Close House, and Mrs Ward, the manager, for allowing me to write about the happenings there; Karen, the projectionist at Cineworld, Daniel Harrison and other managers, for sharing their stories with me, and not just about the cinema; Margaret Pardner, who once worked at Walton Hospital when it was a sanatorium; Dawn Jackson, who runs the Gardeners, and Janet Frith, a member of her staff; Ken and Ann Randall, licensees of both The Rutland and the Royal Oak, also Josh Clarke, manager of the Royal Oak; Diane Watts of the Blue Bell Inn in North Wingfield; National Trust stewards at Hardwick Hall who shared their stories with me; Emma Clarke-Bolton of Sarah Eastel Locations/English Heritage, who kindly arranged for me to photograph inside Bolsover Castle, and Katie at the castle for taking me round; Hayden and Bernice Walker for gathering information about the Holy Trinity church ghost from Madge Eileen Nield; Ann-Marie Knowles, curator of the Chesterfield Museum, for information about Revolution House, and the staff there for their help; Richard Stephens, Head of Leisure Services, for permission to photograph inside Revolution House. Finally, grateful thanks to Philip, my husband, for his support and, above all, technical expertise on the computer.

INTRODUCTION

I have been leading ghost walks around Chesterfield for the past fourteen years. However, I am not a psychic medium, nor have I ever seen a ghost. So how did this all come about?

Whilst in London for a short visit with my husband and younger daughter, we visited Hampton Court. We arrived just in time to be swept along on a guided tour. This experience made the visit so much more enjoyable and interesting. Back in Chesterfield, in the autumn of 1992, I saw a poster advertising a course to train to be a Blue Badge Tourist Guide, a national qualification. I took up the challenge and was accepted onto the course. As one who enjoys talking (and does quite a lot of it) and sharing knowledge, it seemed the ideal occupation; and so it has proved to be.

My association with ghost walks began at the badge presentation ceremony at the Heights of Abraham in Matlock Bath, in May 1993. His Royal Highness the Duke of Gloucester presented our badges in his capacity as the president of the now defunct East Midlands Tourist Board. Bernadette Wainwright, the Tourism Officer for Chesterfield, asked me if I would consider leading ghost walks at Halloween and just before Christmas. There are apparently plenty of ghosts around Chesterfield and the interest was there. Ray Pearson's books about Chesterfield ghosts proved so popular in the local studies library that they themselves kept 'disappearing' and are now kept under lock and key.

There is no doubt that ghost walks are extremely popular in this country. The ghost walks of York and Edinburgh are legendary and many more towns are now running their own ghost trails. There seems to be an insatiable interest in the subject. When I give talks about the ghosts of Chesterfield, people are eager to tell of their own experiences, and those of their friends and relatives. But this interest is not yet so widespread in Europe, as I found out when I was taking a group of French schoolchildren on a walk around Chesterfield one morning. I thought I would liven up the proceedings by telling the story of the mysterious bell ringing at Rose Hill, the house formerly on the site of the Town Hall. There was very little reaction, which I put down to them having been travelling for the previous twenty-four hours. Then the French teacher remarked, rather coolly, 'How very English!' Enquiring if the French were interested in ghost stories, I received the reply, 'Not really'.

But the English embrace them enthusiastically and, in addition to walks organised by the Borough Council, I have taken all sorts of groups around the town: Scouts, Guides, Cubs, Brownies, theatrical societies, birthday party walks for young and old, market traders – the list is long and varied.

The Halloween walks are fun as children very often come along dressed in costumes and with pumpkin lanterns. After an hour the smell of cooking pumpkin lantern lid can become quite powerful. Children never seem to be upset by any of the stories and can sometimes add their own touches. On hearing that a piano on the stage of the theatre began to play all by itself, one small Cub asked calmly, 'What was it playing?' I throw this open to suggestions. My own contribution is *I Ain't Got Nobody* (!). Other offers have been *Ghost Riders in the Sky* and *The Funeral March*.

I deliberately make my approach light-hearted, as I would not like to upset anyone. But I do stress that the stories are real experiences and that many people on the walks have corroborated them and even added their own experiences. To them I am extremely grateful.

Of course, I am almost always asked if I have ever seen a ghost, and the answer is NO. But this does not mean to say that I do not believe in them. Like the rest of the country, I have always been fascinated by the stories and more so by the details given in them which suggest that they are not fabricated. For example, during the time I was undergoing teacher training, we were required to spend two weeks in the summer in another child-related activity. I went to help out at the Hutton Buscel Young Naturalists Centre near Scarborough, which was based in the old rectory. School groups came from all over the country to stay at the rectory and explore the local environment. Children slept in dormitory-style accommodation while the adults were housed in small attic bedrooms, no doubt the servants' quarters in the past. The director told me that those teachers who slept in one particular room consistently complained of being woken in the night. They almost all described the sensation they experienced in the same way: that it was like having bits of cotton wool dropped on their faces. One woman even saw an aura at the end of the bed. Bearing in mind that these people never met each other, for one school group had left before the next one arrived, this is remarkable. What they did not know, and were never told, was that a former rector had hanged himself in that very room.

The fact that people can relate similar experiences in similar circumstances I find good evidence for believing that there really is another dimension which we cannot experience until after death, and that those in that other dimension are free to return.

Some say that spirits remain if they are troubled: some that spirits like to stay in places where they were happy. No doubt this is why George Stephenson continued to visit Tapton House for such a long time. People have told stories of recently deceased relatives revisiting for a last goodbye and to give reassurance that all is well. And people do seem to find comfort in this.

Another fact that leads me to believe in the spirit world, even if I have not experienced it myself, is that ghosts return and inhabit the situation they knew when they were alive. For example, a man told me of seeing a woman walking along Spital Lane. Thinking that it may have been one of the elderly ladies that his wife cared for, he called for her. He then witnessed the figure turn and walk through the wall into the churchyard, at a point where there had formerly been a gate. Similarly, there is the oft-told story of the workman in the Treasurer's House behind the Minster in York. He saw a legion of Roman soldiers, but reported that they were apparently cut off at the knees. He did not know that in Roman times the level of the ground was much lower than the present day. If he had been inventing the story he would, no doubt, have had them fully limbed!

I hope you enjoy this collection of stories of the ghosts of Chesterfield, and the historical notes that precede them. Sometimes the past events in a location will give a possible reason for a supernatural sighting, and sometimes there is no apparent reason, or it has been lost over time. It is always more interesting to put things in their historical context, and Chesterfield has a wealth of history which is worth exploring. The town has long had connections with the Cavendish family, so I make no apology for including some of their properties, and who am I to turn my back on a good story?

I am extremely grateful to all those who have told me their stories over the past few months. I hope I have done them justice. I am absolutely certain that there are more stories out there.

There always are.

CHAPTER ONE

CHURCHES AND CHAPELS

The Crooked Spire

The Chesterfield parish church is the largest in the county and demonstrates the importance of the town in medieval times. Widely known by its nickname, the Crooked Spire, the actual dedication of the church is to St Mary and All Saints. There is documentary evidence from Lincoln Cathedral that William Rufus himself gave the Dean and Chapter of Lincoln permission to appoint a parish priest in Chesterfield in 1100.

The present church was begun in the early thirteenth century at the east end, which, together with the main tower, was dedicated in 1234. Building continued for many years, including a rebuilding of the west front in 1509. During this period occurred the dreadful scourge known as the Black Death. It swept through Europe in the mid-1300s. Many people have suggested that the crookedness of the spire resulted from the death of skilled craftsmen during this period. The use of green wood could have caused the splitting of one of the four main supports of the spire, and the later addition of a huge weight of lead cannot have helped matters. The survey completed at the end of 1999 reported the spire leaning and twisting over 8ft to the south and over 3.5ft to the west.

But despite technical and architectural explanations, the legend still persists that the Devil, flying from Nottingham to Sheffield, sat on the straight spire to rest. His nose was tickled by the incense rising from the interior, which caused him to sneeze. His tail, wrapped round the spire for support, grabbed even tighter, causing the spire to twist. There are even people who claim that the Devil was so amazed to see a virgin marrying in the church that he held tightly to the spire with his tail to lean over and witness this rare event, causing the spire to distort! Apparently the spire will straighten when another virgin marries in the church.

But if the Devil did not appear in Chesterfield in person, it might be argued that he was present in mankind during a murderous attack in the church itself. On 1 January 1434, Sir Henry Pierrepoint and his followers rode to attend Mass in the church. But his avowed enemy, the local landowner and Lord of the Manor, Thomas Foljambe, took the opportunity to settle a few scores. It was a turbulent and lawless period in English history and this would not be an isolated occurrence. Thomas Mogynton, the parish clerk, colluded with Foljambe. He locked the doors to the belfry, vestry and crucifix chapel. Then he rang a church bell as a signal to Foljambe that he had completed his task. With nowhere to hide, the Pierrepoint party was an easy target for the armed men who burst into the church. With swords and arrows in the very church itself, they brought murder and bloodshed to consecrated ground.

But this was not the first time that the church had been at the centre of a conflict. In 1266 there was a battle near the church, which was part of the barons' revolt against King Henry III. In this area the Earl of Derby, Robert Ferrers, was the king's enemy. He was defeated and lost his lands, but a local story has him first hiding in the church to evade capture. History reports that a Chesterfield woman betrayed him, but a *Little Book of Gossip*, printed in the late 1890s, states that the good and virtuous women of Chesterfield would do no such thing!

Imagine then the terror of the Pierrepoint family and retainers, let alone the clergy, as the Foljambes burst into the church. Some must have fled to all corners of the church to escape the slaughter, only to find, of course, that the actions of the parish clerk had trapped them in the nave. Are the ghosts still seeking refuge from the surprise attack on that New Year's Day long ago? Could the phantom footsteps heard in the tower be an echo of that time?

They were heard by one of the bell ringers who also did some maintenance work around the church. But he was not the only one to hear them. Together with his assistant and the archdeacon, he was in the rope room where the ropes from the bells are slung up on to a metal ring called a 'spider' when they are not in use. The three men distinctly heard footsteps coming up the very narrow, twisting stone staircase. It was evening; the church had been locked up for the night. No one else should have been in the building. The footsteps ceased. Summoning up their courage, the three men left the rope room and searched the dark church. They found no evidence of any other persons and the doors were still locked. The bell ringer and his assistant had the very same experience on another evening. Again there was nobody in the church, and all the doors were firmly locked.

Left: *The church of St Mary and All Saints, seen from the Market Place along the High Street.*

Opposite: *The crooked spire with its twist and lean. Did the Devil cause this?*

The north wall of the church where the hooded figure was seen looking through the window.

The bell ringer was alone in the rope room on the third occasion he again heard noises, this time a faint scrabbling in the room above him where he had just been to complete some work on the clock mechanism. One of the bell ropes began to shake gently. This time his nerve gave way and he summoned the police. Two constables and a sergeant turned up. Although they searched the tower and the rest of the church they found no evidence of human activity On returning to the rope room they discovered the culprit, for a tiny dead sparrow lay on the floor. Its death fluttering had been the cause of the faint noise above the ceiling. It had then knocked against the rope, causing it to move, before falling though the hole to be discovered by the (understandably) nervous bell ringer and the police. Or could it have been the blond, brown-robed monk who appeared to a woman when she visited the spire one day? She became so nervous of the height when climbing the narrow, stone spiral steps that she 'froze'. She completed her visit safely thanks to the calming influence of the holy figure.

One evening, two women were crossing the churchyard using a path that passes the west end of the church. There was a swirling mist covering the ground. Glancing to the right, they both noticed a figure by the church wall apparently peering in through one of the windows.

He wore a brown hooded robe, and as he turned his head towards them they realised that he had no face. Both got the impression that the robe was like that of a monk.

The following week, taking the same path behind the church, the two women dared themselves to look at the place where they had seen the figure. This time there was no mist. They noted, to their dismay, that at that particular spot it would have been impossible for a human being to stand and stare through the window. Between the churchyard and the north wall of the church is a deep drainage channel. The stone retaining wall is well over 3ft high and the gap between it and the church wall is over 5ft. wide

Two choirboys, one of whom was a senior chorister, saw a more formless figure inside the church. They were working in the walk-in music store just off the vestry. All the choristers had to take turns in keeping the store tidy and repair any books that were damaged. One boy came out of the store, closely followed by the other, and both were astonished to see a featureless shape

The deep, wide gulley that would prevent any human being standing close to the wall.

hovering in the vestry. Its shroud-like white shape was clearly visible against the blue curtain, which was drawn across the vestments hanging on hooks on the wall. The figure moved slowly towards the solid door, through which it passed with ease.

When one of the boys was involved with an ouija board, he was tempted to ask it if he had ever seen a ghost. The answer was *Yes*. He then asked where he had seen one. The 'spirit' spelt out *in church*. 'What was the name of the ghost?' he asked. *Bella Foljambe* was the reply.

The tomb of Isabella Foljambe is just to the right of the High Altar in the church of St Mary and All Saints.

Holy Trinity Church

Chesterfield began to expand in the late eighteenth century. By the beginning of the nineteenth it became obvious that the parish church was too small for the growing population. Also, many of the pews at the parish church were private, being used by wealthy local families. The 6th Duke of Devonshire gave land for the building of what was termed a 'free' church, meaning that the pews were available to all. The resulting Holy Trinity was opened in 1838. The church is on Newbold Road with the churchyard extending to Sheffield Road. Looking back from the gates giving access to Sheffield Road, one can see the beautiful stained-glass east window given by Robert, George Stephenson's son, in memory of his father. The only other memorial to him is within the church, a floor plaque with the simple initials G.S. and the year of his death, 1848.

Situated as it is between two main roads, the churchyard has been used as a shortcut for many years. In 1927, one ten year old, Madge, was to have a very strange experience using the path past the church. She was a pupil at St Helen's Kindergarten, but lived a little way away in Whittington Moor. She travelled by bus, which took her to the top of Sheffield Road.

Holy Trinity church on Newbold Road. George Stephenson is buried here.

As she was rather late one November morning, she decided to take a shortcut through St Trinity churchyard. She entered through the wrought-iron gates noting that only the left-hand gate was open. Madge hurried along the path, but about halfway up she turned round and looked back towards the gate. To this day she cannot explain the reason why she did so. By the entrance she saw a 'grey, misty shape' apparently leaning against one gatepost. The shape had no clear outline but was a figure about the size of a small adult. It was not transparent. As she watched, it slowly disappeared. Then, remembering the lateness of the hour, she hurried on up the path to school. Even in her late eighties, Madge remembers the event clearly. She was not frightened, just puzzled.

Another reported sighting of a figure in the churchyard again seems not to have caused fear, just bewilderment. During the Second World War there was a complete blackout to prevent bombers recognising targets. So, to be on night duty, travelling without benefit of street and house lighting, must have been rather eerie. This was the lot of a young man who worked as a fireman on the LMS Railway. As he also lived in Whittington Moor, like young Madge, he had to cycle across the town using Sheffield Road as part of his route to the engine sheds in Hasland. His route took him past Holy Trinity churchyard.

On one journey, as he was passing the gates of the churchyard, he saw, despite the lack of light, the figure of a woman in a white dress. It was 2.30 a.m. No doubt he was wondering why she was all alone when most people were sound asleep in their beds. He stopped to enquire if she was all right, but she did not reply, merely disappearing into the trees. Afraid of being late for work, he did not linger. Arriving safely he told his workmates that he thought he had seen a ghost. They just laughed at him.

The gates to the churchyard of Holy Trinity church on Sheffield Road. A young girl saw a ghost leaning against one of the posts.

He cycled to work again the following night, or rather morning, for he was a little earlier at 2.00 a.m. Again he saw the woman standing at the gates of the church. This time she held a crucifix in her hand. Despite his suspicion that she might be a ghost, or because of it, he again stopped. He asked if she had been there the previous morning and she replied that she had. In answer to his repeated enquiry if she was all right, she assured him that she was. When asked why she had not spoken last time they met, she merely made the excuse that she was a little deaf. The brief encounter was over.

Had the fireman seen a ghost? He was never sure, but certainly the appearance of a lady in white, holding a crucifix in a churchyard at that time in the morning had to have been one of the strangest events of his life.

Eyre Chapel

Just off Newbold Road, behind the Nags Head public house, is one of Chesterfield's best-kept religious secrets. Only the brown information sign saying Eyre chapel alerts an observant visitor to its presence. The chapel is tiny compared to the grandeur of the parish church. Its stone walls and typical Derbyshire stone slab roof, with pinnacles at each corner, enclose a space measuring a mere 36ft by 16ft. Around it are the grassy remains of a graveyard. Thankfully, the Civic Society has stepped in to restore the chapel once again and they hold their meetings there.

The Nags Head at Newbold with the Eyre chapel hidden away behind.

The tiny Eyre chapel. It has been restored and the vault firmly sealed to prevent further misdeeds.

To be near Eyre chapel, despite its proximity to a busy road, is to take a step back in time. The parish of Newbold featured in the Domesday Book and was of more importance at that time than Chesterfield. Eyre chapel was built as a chapel of ease in the thirteenth century. It was then dedicated to St Martin. A chapel of ease was built in outlying areas where it was too difficult for the people to get to the local church. They were, in effect, assistant churches.

The chapel then became associated with the Eyre family. The Eyres came over with William the Conqueror, and, in common with many other local families, gained their lands as direct gifts from William I. The Eyres remained a prominent Roman Catholic family well into the era of religious history that saw many people denouncing their faith in the face of persecution. They became a shelter for recusants (those refusing to be dictated to by authority) at a time when a change of monarchy often meant a change of religion.

Over the centuries the general population experienced much turbulence during their religious lives. So too did this diminutive place of worship, which may account for the strange sights and sounds seen and heard around it.

The chapel was restored in 1686 when James II decreed that Roman Catholics could worship in public, yet two years later it was ransacked by a mob. Could this have been because in that year, 1688, the Glorious Revolution had brought a Protestant monarchy, for good, in the form of William and Mary? (See Revolution House.)

Tombstones were destroyed at this time, and were even taken to be incorporated in local buildings. Then the chapel became a cowshed for a while. This was not an unusual use for such a building; consecrated places were considered a safe place in which to keep livestock. Padley chapel near Grindleford (another Catholic place of worship) suffered the same fate. The Eyre family restored the chapel in 1885, but it again fell into disrepair to be further restored and then used for services until 1965, when it was again left deserted.

Then came a shocking desecration of this centuries-old building. In 1967 thieves broke into the chapel and gained entry to the Eyre family vault beneath the flagstone floor, breaking their way through over 3ft of stone. The vault had been created just over a hundred years earlier, when the remains of fourteen of the Eyre family members had been brought in from the graveyard. More disturbing still, a table and candles had been set up above the vault as if to prepare for a Black Mass, a perverse sign of Devil worship in this place of God. The nearby Peak District, well known for being one of the most haunted areas in the country, was also the site of Pagan practices quite late on in the history of religion. In fact, many of the local customs appear to have Pagan influences. The Well Dressings, almost entirely unique to the county, may have their origins in the Roman worship of wells and fountains. The Castleton Garland Ceremony, when the Garland King wears a 'wicker cage' of flowers, may have echoes of a fertility rite, although it now 'pretends' to celebrate the Restoration of the monarchy in 1660. The football in the Ashbourne Football Game may well have started off as a sacrificial severed head.

People living in the nearby Nags Head public house have also experienced what they described as supernatural sounds, which they attributed to the ancient chapel. Chanting has been heard and robed figures have been seen in the area of the two buildings.

So, does the troubled history of the chapel account for the supernatural happenings around it? Or was it the blatant desecration of a Christian site with echoes of Derbyshire's Pagan past which caused people to see strange lights around the chapel and the indistinct shape of a hooded figure? The manor of Newbold was once the holding of a religious house. Did monks come to visit? Or, Heaven forbid, are these figures and sounds from a pre-Christian era?

The front of Livingstone's nightclub, formerly Holywell Cross church. Was a ghost caught on CCTV?

Hollywell Cross Church (now Livingstone's Nightclub)

The former Methodist chapel, turreted and built from attractive blue and red brick, is not far from the old Royal Hospital. It faces on to the large Hollywell Cross car park to the east of the market. (There was indeed a Holy Well, situated down Sheffield Road past the old Grammar School buildings.) The chapel dates from 1881.

When the chapel was still a place of worship, some of the congregation had got together to do some decorating in the main body of the building. Above them was a balcony on which the organ was situated. The balcony could be accessed from either side by doors. As the group got on with painting, they suddenly experienced a drop in temperature. Sensing a presence, they looked towards the organ balcony. Slowly the door on the left opened and a shadowy figure drifted towards the right-hand door through which it exited. This apparently was a regular occurrence between 9.00 p.m. and 10.00 p.m.

When the chapel became redundant as a place of worship, it became a multi-purpose building including the YMCA. The central hall was split into two levels. One evening, a group of four young men who had formed a rock group had been using the venue to rehearse. After they had finished, three remained behind to pack up the equipment. Suddenly there was a drop in temperature and one of the young men fell into a trance-like state. During it, he seemed to be commenting on a sermon as if he were the member of a congregation. Somehow, he had 'tapped in' to the previous life of the chapel. As the temperature returned to normal he recovered, but could not remember what had happened.

One evening, the building was deserted except for a few members of staff. All the doors were locked. So, when a female member of staff went into the kitchen to fetch a bottle of milk, she was startled to see the figure of a man dressed in an old mackintosh and wearing a hat. The caretakers searched the building but could find no intruder and the doors were all found to be still locked. The figure has in fact been seen many times and is referred to as 'Mickey' or 'Ickey', and is thought to be the ghost of an earlier caretaker. On another occasion, a man thought he was being followed down a corridor. On turning he found it was deserted, but he described the footsteps as sounding like those of a woman, so 'Mickey' may not be alone.

Janet, who works at the Gardener's in Glumangate, has also worked at Livingstone's as a cleaner. As she and her colleagues were taking a coffee break near the main dance floor, there was a sudden drop in temperature, as experienced by the young men years before. She reports seeing a figure dressed in dark clothes, 'almost like a priest', and it was as if he 'jumped inside me', she said. Her colleagues noted that she went deathly white.

The ghosts of the old Hollywell Cross chapel had better watch out, for it is not only human eyes that can catch sight of them these days; a CCTV camera also caught a spectre in the VIP area. The fun of haunting must be to access all areas, regardless of status.

The Ragged School

Dwarfed by the bulk of the multi-storey car park between Beetwell Street and Markham Road is a small building still known as the Ragged School. The building is currently used as a place of worship. Its original address was Wheeldon Lane, most of which is now covered up by the car park. Originally Wheeldon Lane ran up to the market place emerging opposite the Market Hall where Joplin's public house is now situated. This part of the town, between the market place and the river Hipper, was very much a poor slum area, which has now been cleared away.

Before the present building occupied the site, there was a carpet factory. In its time the Ragged School building, probably dating from 1837, was itself a lace factory, and then the premises of a tobacco and pipe manufacturer. The current name was acquired when a Ragged School opened in 1878. Prior to this, the building was used as a lodging house, which acquired such a poor reputation that it was closed down. These schools provided a basic education for poor children, who, being at work, could only attend on Sundays. The lessons were followed by a church service. Hundreds of children benefited from this wonderful idea. The teachers were all volunteers.

The building gained yet another function when it was taken over by the Ministry of Defence in 1914. The Lancashire Fusiliers moved in, and the children and teachers move out to the Hipper Street School (now demolished) for eight months.

With so much human activity over the years, it seems inevitable that traces of it should remain in the strange occurrences in the building. Locked doors with latch-type handles have been heard to open and close, accompanied by the sound of echoing footsteps. Considering that this building was once used for manufacturing, it should come as no surprise that the sound of humming machinery has been recorded.

The poor area of the town, formerly known as the Dog Kennels, has changed radically since the Ragged School took in the local children to give them an education.

The Ragged School has had many uses over the years. The variety of ghosts may reflect its past.

Whispering has also been heard. Some thought that they identified the word 'colonel' among others. Was this perhaps an echo of the First World War MOD days? Or maybe the word was 'kennel'. The small room above the porch was called the Dog Kennel, and the slum area was known as the Dog Kennels. How many of the children from that area began their education at the Ragged School, only to perish in the mud of the trenches?

But the haunting of this old building is not in sound alone; a shadowy figure has also been seen in the building. Emerging from smoke, with flashes of light, the ethereal shape of an emaciated woman has been seen more than once, but each time for only a few seconds. As the temperature drops, she moves forward tentatively, with apparently no legs. This is because the floor level has been raised so she, from a former era, must be walking on the original floor level. Could she have been one of the volunteer teachers at the Ragged School?

The route to Ramcroft Mine from Heath is beautiful in sunlight, but the walk to work became so frightening that miners would not go alone.

The Twin Oaks Motel was formerly miners' cottages for the Ramcroft Colliery.

Heath Old Church

The village of Heath (originally 'lunt', meaning clearing in the woodland) lies a very short distance from Junction 29 of the M1. But it retains a peaceful, docile quality that earned it the nickname of 'Dozy Heath' for many years. The settlement was mentioned in the Domesday Book, and for 300 years it was owned by the Cistercian monks of Geronden Abbey. Past owners have also included the Savages of Stainsby and Bess of Hardwick. Whilst the surrounding land provided a very good source of income in farming, what lay beneath the land was to prove far more valuable, because rich coal seams were found in the Vale of Scarsdale to the east. The Ramcroft Colliery was established in the late nineteenth century. It was to provide coal for the war effort from 1914 onwards, and then, after a lull, to become productive again to provide coal for the Second World War. The colliery closed in 1966.

The ruins of Heath old church, rebuilt as a mortuary chapel, seen from the gateway. It seems peaceful, but the M1 traffic roars past close by.

The ruined walls of Heath old church, on which the miners would see the White Lady 'walking'.

Inside the ruins of the former Heath parish church, which was replaced in the mid-nineteenth century.

Miners who lived in Heath went to work along Ramcroft Lane, which passed the ruins of Heath's original old church. It had been replaced in 1852. Other miners lived in the settlement of purpose-built cottages which, together with two villas for the under-managers, bore the name of Ramcroft. The M1 now separates Heath and the former Ramcroft, although a tunnel under the motorway still connects them. The cottages and villas were bought in the early 1980s and converted into the Twin Oaks Motel and restaurant, thus preserving some of the history of the area. The ruins of the old church can be found by taking the small lane on the left immediately before the slip road on to the M1 North. The walls of the tiny, 500-year-old church stand quietly amongst the bluebells in the overgrown graveyard, whilst the traffic of the twenty-first century rushes by.

Ramcroft Lane was a well-trodden route to the colliery but it was dark at night and normally deserted. Two miners, on their way to work, were therefore startled to see a woman in a white dress standing on a stone wall that had been part of the old church. They did not recognise her, but their prime concern was for her safety as the wall was in a poor state of repair and dangerous. As they drew nearer to the beautiful woman, they noted, to their horror, that she was a transparent phantom. As the two miners watched, she began to float around the walls of the old church. Screaming with terror they fled to the colliery where they related their ghostly experience.

Ramcroft Colliery itself was haunted, as were others in the area. Mostly they were the ghosts of long-dead miners. The Bolsover Colliery ghost had a candle burning on the front of his helmet instead of a lamp. He asked the way to the pit shaft, and on being taken there, walked straight through a locked door. The Shirebrook ghost was that of a recently dead miner, and the Silver Hill ghost calmly asked for his snap box to be returned as he had left it in the cage. The deputy agreed before realising that the 'man' was no longer present. But the ghostly presence of former colleagues, hundreds of feet below ground in the darkness of the mine, was not only less alarming than the White Lady of Heath ruins, but positively welcomed. For the appearance of long-dead miners is generally regarded as a warning of danger, and there are many instances of miners owing their lives to the appearance of such figures. But the White Lady was a different thing altogether. She was seen often, occasionally floating around the churchyard with its ancient tombstones, and sometimes wafting along the tops of the walls surrounding the churchyard. The miners began to dread using the lane and took to walking along it in small groups, rather than alone or with one companion.

Was she a long-dead miner's wife looking for her husband, or a widow mourning the loss of a loved one in the ancient churchyard?

The sightings of the phantom White Lady of Ramcroft Lane ceased following the closure of the mine.

North Wingfield Churchyard

The industry-blackened, 500-year-old stones of St Lawrence's church stand proudly on the hill overlooking the main railway line to London. The interior boasts much of interest, fourteenth-century tracery beam work, a Norman arch and ancient font. In the chancel can be found effigies of knights in chain mail, members of the Deincourt family who had connections with the manor of Sutton Scarsdale. The local secondary school bears the name 'Deincourt'. The 80ft church tower has seen the village grow from a small farming community with some coal and iron-stone mining to a larger community involved with the increased coal mining, and related industries, in the area. Although the coal mining has now gone, the legacy remains in the walks known as the Five Pits Trail.

The churchyard of North Wingfield church, where the 'Mad Monk' was encountered.

Two ghosts have been seen in the area, but a particularly disturbing one is the mad monk. He appears in St Lawrence's churchyard at precisely 2.30 a.m. Only once was he seen during the day when he 'walked' through a small gate, opening it first, and then drifted towards the churchyard. But members of a paranormal research team had a very unnerving experience in the early morning presence of this spectre. The group had an extremely uncomfortable feeling when he appeared and all members had an urge to flee the churchyard. One of the group was very badly affected. Later he described how he had felt a great force pressing on him. His companions saw him shaking with cold and the blood drained from his face. Strangest of all, he began to chant in Latin, a language he had never learned, but one that would be well known to a medieval monk. His ordeal lasted ten minutes. Fortunately the group knew how to call for spiritual help and they were released. Leaving the churchyard hurriedly, they vowed never to return.

North Wingfield seems to specialise in ecclesiastical ghosts, for a nun has been seen in another part of the village called Slack Lane. Shire Lane, just off Slack Lane, was at one time the site of a convent.

About thirty years ago, a gentleman was returning from an evening out in the pub. His walk home took him along Slack Lane. (Slack is a local dialect name for a hollow.) To his surprise, for it was a bitter winter night, he saw a nun coming towards him. As she passed him she seemed to be floating rather than walking, and in her presence the man felt cold and uncomfortable. He turned to look at her again after she had passed, and that is when he saw her slowly dissolve away. He arrived home to his wife in a great state of agitation and white as the proverbial sheet. One particular thing he could remember about her was that she was wearing spectacles. His friends made fun of him when he told them about his encounter. The couple moved away, but one New Year's Eve they chanced to meet some former neighbours from Slack Lane. One of them confessed that he had also seen the ghostly nun, and, yes, he too had noticed that she was wearing spectacles!

Barrow Hill Rectory/School House

The Staveley area abounded in iron and coal reserves, hence the growth of the Staveley Works that dominated both the surroundings and the lives of the people. At its height, in the fifties, the Staveley Coal & Iron Company may have employed around ninety per cent of the population in the works and the collieries. The nearby settlement, called Barrow Hill, obtained its name from the ironmaster who founded it. Mr Richard Barrow built extensively to house his workers. Two hundred houses, with water laid on, were built in blocks of three, hence their local name 'The Blocks'. A school was built in 1856. Barrow Hill has seen much demolition and rebuilding; one of the places to disappear being the rectory/school house. But the stories associated with it live on.

Ghostly footsteps, doors opening and closing, a chilly atmosphere and lights going on and off seem to be the normal haunting fare for spirits, and so it was in the old Barrow Hill Rectory, but it can boast more unusual, yet equally frightening, happenings.

The extremely disturbing atmosphere in the bathroom upset many visitors. Some said they had a choking sensation in the room, and their only thought was to get out as swiftly as possible. This may be explained by the information that a rather eccentric lady had lived in the house at one time. She had dyed her hair bright green and dyed her poodle to match. They must have made a strange and colourful pair. Tragically, the woman died as a result of having a fit whilst she was taking a bath.

But she, and the poodle, may well have revisited their home in the form of a mist that was seen near a spiral staircase, for the mist was a distinct green.

All Saints Church, Ashover

Hidden away in the Amber Valley to the west of the town centre is Ashover, the second largest parish in the country, covering fifteen square miles with fifty-five miles of roads. What now appears to be a rural idyll was once a busy community involved in lead mining, quarrying and farming.

The ancient and beautiful church, begun in 1350, has many interesting features – and ghosts. Within the church is a lead font, with figures around it, which are thought to be the apostles. It is very rare, as there are fewer than thirty left in the country. Many suffered the fate of being melted down for bullets during the Civil War, much as iron railings were recycled during the Second World War. The tomb of the Babington family dates from 1511 and has above it, on the wall, a 'palimpsest'. The word is Greek for 'twice written', and indeed the flap of hinged metal is engraved on both sides. It is the only brass palimpsest in the country

The ghost seen within the church, in the north aisle, was that of a headless woman. This sighting occurred at 8.00 p.m. in the evening and must have been a great shock. As the last sighting was in 1890 it can be assumed that local residents, on hearing about it, were reminded of a dreadful murder and suicide, fifty years previously.

All Saints church, Ashover; a delightful village just west of Chesterfield.

The empty coffin at the west end of the church. It is no longer possible to walk around it, but you can still lie down in it – if you dare!

In June 1841, a farmer named John Towndrow killed his wife in a frenzied attack with a hammer. But this was not to be the end; he then chopped off her head before cutting his own throat. After a local jury deliberated, he was buried in the churchyard late in the evening without his shoes. What dreadful provocation could have prompted such a tragedy? Is it any wonder that the poor spectre looked for sanctuary in the church?

A head, or rather a skull, features in another story centred on Ashover and the church. During a party at Stubben Edge Hall, close to the village, a young man took up a challenge to acquire a skull from the local churchyard. This was 1850 and such wild pranks were not unknown. The display of a skull would not have upset people too much in an age when collecting bizarre objects was a hobby! The long-dead owner of the skull, disturbed during its theft from the grave, took to wandering the churchyard.

The skull was eventually returned in 1889 when building work was being undertaken at the hall and it came to light.

That two people should have their skulls taken from their bodies, one in life and one in death, in the same century in the same village must be something of a record. Is it any wonder that a headless spectre was seen in the church? But a year after the return of the skull, people no longer saw the headless ghost, so rest came at last to the decapitated. The question remains if they were the same person. It would seem to be the nastiest of pranks to take the skull of the murdered farmer's wife.

In the past, if you wished to frighten yourself, and many people did, you could go and find the centuries-old stone coffin outside the church. The tradition was to walk around the coffin three times, and then lie down in it with your eyes closed. Those who did this all reported hearing faint noises, which then grew louder, followed by the rattling of chains. One man who lay in the coffin as a boy did hear noises, but his friend did not, perhaps because he was not a local. The coffin has now been moved close up against the church wall so that it is no longer possible to walk around it. But you can still lie down in it. It is amazing how many visitors to the county love to take photographs of each other standing in the stone coffins resting upright against the west wall of Bakewell church. Offered the chance to do the same in a modern coffin with satin lining they might well refuse!

CHAPTER TWO

HOSPITALS

Ashgate Hospice

The hospice lies to the west of the town centre, as suburbia gives way to the countryside, and the hills of the Peak District beckon. It is a peaceful place for those who need peace at a troubled time in their lives. The new wing is a credit to the fundraisers and architects, but the old buildings on the site are equally interesting and steeped in history.

The Barnes family, from nearby Old Brampton, built the original residence in 1647. The low stone-built house looks fairly modest, but the extension, with the date stone DB 1768, is a much grander affair. The two three-part Venetian windows, with semi-circular windows above, show that the family was wealthy and wanted to build in the latest grand style. This family also needed the room; John Barnes and his second wife increased the family from eight children to sixteen! A Victorian coach house (1861) completes the mixture of buildings on the site.

The original business of this successful yeoman family included a windmill for crushing bones for fertiliser. But a hundred years later they owned coal seams at Barlow and an iron works at Stonegravels. Three of the sons of John Gorrell Barnes had a shipping business in Liverpool by the early years of the nineteenth century. Their brother, Alfred, went to train as an engineer at George Stephenson's works. Sadly, he had to give this up because of a weak heart, but he went on to run the Grassmoor Colliery Company. Alfred's son, Edwin, persuaded other coal owners to contribute to another ward for the Royal Hospital in the town after the First World War. The completed ward bore the name 'Barnes', as does its successor in the new Royal Hospital at Calow. In 1929 Arthur Barnes installed the first pithead baths in Derbyshire.

This remarkable, but little known, family occupied the Ashgate estate for nearly 300 years. They now live in the south of the country. The hospice has a picture of the house painted by Joy Barnes in 1989. It commemorates the last owner, Thomas Harold Barnes T.D. (1896-1971), Lieutenant Colonel of the 2nd Derbyshire Yeomanry. There are also brass plaques in Old Brampton church commemorating members of this remarkable family.

During the First World War, the house became a hospital for wounded soldiers. The buildings were taken over by the RASC (Royal Army Service Corps, concerned with logistics) during the Second World War. The Barnes family connection with the estate then ceased. Derbyshire District Council then aquired the site and converted the buildings to provide hostel accommodation for refugees from Tunbridge Wells. Eventually, the Chesterfield and North Derbyshire Royal Hospital used the site as an annexe for patients who were convalescing.

An appeal launched in June 1985 saw the start of the hospice movement in Chesterfield and the continuation of the caring which has gone on around this complex of old and new buildings for ninety years.

With such a long history associated with the traumas of life, it is not surprising that the old buildings have had, and are still having, their fair share of strange and puzzling events. During one of the periods when the buildings were used as a hospital annexe, a nurse was concerned at the sight of a patient at the far end of a ward putting on his dressing gown. It was evening and he was meant to be in bed. But as she approached the man to ask why he was getting up, he vanished.

One patient had been a particular favourite of the nurses. His presence stayed with them when he died, as they often heard his footsteps at night. They had been quite distinctive, so when the staff heard the footsteps they knew that their former patient had not entirely moved on. A ghost who made less noise, but could be seen distinctly, was a man in Edwardian clothes who was frequently spotted in the reception, near a large fireplace.

The original buildings in which the Barnes family lived. The site is now occupied by Ashgate Hospice, and these buildings are used as offices.

The date stone on the extension to the original buildings.

The eighteenth-century buildings belong to the hospice. The room under the left-hand chimney was the scene of a haunting.

A fireplace also featured in another story. Three young male patients were chatting to a nurse. One of them asked if she had been on duty the previous evening, as he thought he had seen her. She replied that she had not. But another young man intervened to say that the nurse he had seen had looked quite different; she had been wearing a long grey dress. The third man then spoke up to say that he also had seen the 'nurse' in the long grey dress, and that he had watched as she vanished by walking into the fireplace.

A long grey dress could well have been the uniform of nurses during the First World War when wounded soldiers were cared for at Ashgate. Perhaps the ghost nurse thought that the three convalescing young men were like her patients long ago.

Today the staff live with the knowledge that they are 'not alone' even when they think they are! Two people, Theresa and Pam, have had their names called out. Another member of staff was with Pam when they both heard the ghost call out 'Paaaam' in a drawn-out voice, although there was no one nearby. The voice repeated its call, 'Paaaam', and the temperature dropped for no apparent reason. A cold spot also occurs in the corridor between two of the bays, and one is especially evident in a cupboard which all refer to as 'Victoria's Cupboard'. This is a walk-in storage area just off a large office in the eighteenth-century extension. It has such a strange atmosphere that many people hate to go in there.

They also report that this old part of the hospice complex seems to have a permanent aura, especially at night. Footsteps are often heard approaching; but no one arrives. A member of staff was fumbling for a light switch one evening in a dark corridor when she felt a hand brush across her hair. One particular ghost has a sense of humour. Vacuuming the Red Stairs, the staff name for the beautiful cantilevered oak staircase with red carpet, one of the housekeepers heard a laugh behind her. It was 7.00 a.m. and there was nobody else in the area. This particular spirit was rude enough to laugh when a woman tripped on that same carpet. Or did she trip over a ghostly foot?

With a pink haze in the kitchen corridor, and swirling lights near the conservatory, one might be forgiven for thinking that the ghosts have become shy and do not wish to show themselves. Not so. A nurse in a 'Crimean' uniform has been seen and a boy, age unspecified, was seen in

Above left: *The former fireplace into which a ghostly figure vanished. It now houses a safe.*

Above right: *Victoria's cupboard, just off one of the main offices, is a 'cold spot'. Many staff hate to go in there because of the 'strange atmosphere'.*

his vest and pants before he disappeared. Two builders have good reason to remember the work they did on converting the old buildings to their present use. They looked up from their task to see what they described as a 'Victorian lady'. But they saw only her torso, no legs. They left the premises, never to return.

Perhaps the most touching story is of a ghost with only a slight connection to the property. As a patient lay dying, staff saw a dog on the bed. The man died and the dog disappeared. It was later learned that the patient's dog, which was at home, had died just before its master.

Chesterfield and North Derbyshire Royal Hospital

The imposing building, which was built as the town's first 'proper' hospital, is situated on the corner of Durrant Street and overlooks Hollywell Cross car park. The heir to the Chatsworth estate, the Marquis of Hartington, opened it in 1859. Now an office building, it has been sympathetically extended to the rear. The previous 'hospital' was in St Mary's Gate, near the church, but it had only six beds and many, many outpatients as it was much cheaper to be the latter. The new hospital doubled the number of hospital in-patient beds in the town – to twelve! These were for surgical cases only. Medical wards would follow only in the late nineteenth century. The hospital received the 'Royal' in its title in 1917 in recognition of the efforts of the townspeople in raising money to pay off the building debts.

The former Chesterfield and North Derbyshire Royal Hospital, now offices. The children's ward, Nightingale, was on the top floor on the left-hand side.

On the top floor at the northern end of the building was Nightingale Ward, the ward for children and babies. Over the years many staff have commented on the fact that this ward had a peculiar atmosphere, especially where the babies were cared for. One ex-nurse said that the air always felt chilly, even though the babies themselves were warm. Doors opened and shut on their own on this ward and footsteps were heard with shadows seeming to accompany the sound. They tried to keep Nightingale Ward well staffed as, from time to time, nurses left, unable to cope with the strange happenings. More seriously, the nurses would find that the oxygen cylinders, which were kept in the ward, had had their settings altered without the intervention of the medical staff. So frequently did this occur that a porter was asked to sit by the cylinders to keep an eye on them. This seemed like quite a stress-free job until a spanner, used to adjust the valve on the top of the cylinders, raised itself up from the table and floated across the room towards him! The porter fled.

There may be an explanation for all these happenings in the fact that a nurse once accidentally caused the death of a baby by administering the wrong dose of oxygen. She subsequently committed suicide at the hospital.

But there have been many more hauntings in other parts of the hospital. Staff on night duty in the Coronary Unit frequently heard footsteps as if doctors were hurrying to the unit, but no one arrived. A doctor saw a patient in a surgical gown walking along a corridor. He followed the man, curious to know why he was wandering about out of bed. Losing sight of the figure momentarily as he went round a corner, the doctor was amazed to find that he had disappeared completely on a corridor with no exits.

One day, it was the sad duty of a porter to accompany two people to the mortuary to identify a body. He went in first to see that all was prepared, and was shocked to see a man sitting up on one of the two trolleys there. He was so sure that it was a real person that he questioned his right to be there without authority. But the man merely smiled, floated up from the trolley and passed through the wall. The porter left his job as he felt he could no longer enter the mortuary.

A former side ward, which was being used as a storeroom, was the scene of another strange disappearance. Passing the entrance, a Sister was surprised and annoyed to come across a patient sitting in a wheelchair in the midst of all the stored equipment. Furious at this apparent neglect of a patient, the Sister rushed to the main ward and ordered that he be retrieved immediately. Although the side ward was seconds away, by the time the staff got there the man had gone, but the wheelchair remained. Was it a ghost, or a miracle cure?

But perhaps the strangest stories revolve around dying patients. Two nurses on night duty were in the ward office about 4.30 a.m. When they heard voices, as if two patients were talking, they hurried to investigate. Over the bed in the corner there was what they could only describe as a mist or fog. Sadly the patient in that bed had died. The 'mist' then cleared, even though there was no draught, which would have made it do just that in ordinary circumstances.

One of the two nurses was again on night duty when she had been told to keep an eye on a very sick patient who was not expected to last the night. The bed had been partially screened for privacy and, as the nurse went by on her duties, she noticed that there was a visitor by the bed. Although it was outside visiting hours, she assumed that the dying patient had been granted the special privilege of a visitor. She continued to see the visitor who each time gave a rather sad smile.

As the night wore on, it occurred to her that the naval uniform of the visitor was somewhat old-fashioned. It had epaulettes with gold-braided tassels, which she was sure were not on modern uniforms. Later, going to check on the patient's condition, which had worsened, the nurse found that the 'visitor' had apparently left. But he had not gone far. Sighting him at the end of the ward, still with that sad smile, she hurried towards him eager to satisfy her curiosity and allay her fears. But the naval officer with the sad smile evaporated away before her very eyes. As the patient later died, the nurse was left to wander if she had seen a long-dead spirit from the 'other world' sent to comfort the patient during his final hours and accompany him on his onward journey. Had the voices she had heard in the previous experience, when the mist had appeared over the bed, also been manifestations of spirits from beyond the grave? We may never know for sure.

Walton Hospital

To the south of the town, facing countryside and the healing rays of the sun (when it shines), there is a collection of cream-coloured low-rise buildings. This hospital, then called the Derby County Sanatorium, was designed specifically for the treatment of tuberculosis. The 100-bed unit was built on a greenfield site and cost £22,000. By the 1930s the building was known as Walton Sanatorium, or just 'the San'.

In the days before antibiotics, fresh air was used as a cure for TB. Wards were built with sides that could be opened. 'Wrap up warmly and breathe deeply' was the order of the day. Light and air poured in through the ceiling windows as well as the French windows, which were left open in all weathers. In order to effect a cure the fresh air had to circulate for as long as possible, so when visitors came, they had to huddle into their overcoats, whilst the patients avoided the worst of the elements by being warmly tucked into their beds. Snow would sometimes land on the beds, but unless it became really bad, the French windows stayed firmly open.

After the Second World War, the antibiotic streptomycin was the main weapon in the fight against TB. But many died from this terrible disease, some even had to have thoracic surgery in the long, low building known as Barwise Ward. How nervous the patients must have felt in that ward, so is it any wonder that phantom footsteps were heard padding along the corridors towards the bathroom, and bells could be heard ringing from beds that were no longer occupied?

Formerly a sanatorium, Walton Hospital to the south-east of the town still has open views over the countryside.

Barwise Ward, where footsteps were heard padding along to the bathroom and bells rang from empty beds.

Although no longer a sanatorium, there are still echoes of the past. A gentleman spent a short spell in Walton Hospital, as it is now called. He related to his wife how he had been standing at the washbasin when he felt a presence behind him and heard a voice saying, 'You're going to be alright.' He turned round to see a nurse in old-fashioned clothing complete with apron and starched hat. Before he could respond the figure had gone. He related all this to one of the staff, who merely responded, 'Oh, you've seen her too, have you?' in a matter-of-fact way which seemed to indicate she was a regular visitor. The man's wife was the most astounded of all for, as she remarked, how could her husband have heard the phantom nurse's comment when was very deaf?!

CHAPTER THREE

HOUSES GREAT AND SMALL

Bradbury Hall

The familiar late nineteenth-century frontage of Bradbury Hall on Chatsworth Road is no more, having recently been demolished. The older building on the site, which was later extended, was called Field House. Many well-known families occupied this house during the nineteenth century. The first was John Smith, son of the founder of the Griffin Iron works, then Francis Frith who was to become internationally known as a photographer. The images of Victorian England, which he created, are still used today in books and displays.

The house was rented in 1852, and then later bought by William Bradbury Robinson. In 1839 his father, John Bradbury Robinson, had founded the packaging manufacturing company that developed into one of the most important industries in the town. Boxes for pills were amongst their early products. The business diversified and became the first company in the world to manufacture surgical dressings at Wheatbridge Mills. William's son, Sir Robert Robinson, was awarded the Nobel Prize for chemistry in 1947, being one of the foremost organic chemists of his time. He is buried in Westminster Abbey. The company, Robinson & Sons, bought Field House in 1928 and added further buildings. It became a canteen and social welfare club for the hundreds of employees.

But there were unquiet spirits in Bradbury Hall. They had been known to throw objects from shelves in the bars. Sometimes objects from the back of the shelves fell to the floor and smashed, whilst those at the front remained undisturbed. One man who witnessed a spectral figure was a plumber called to do some work in the attic. The caretaker became concerned about the plumber as he failed to appear for a promised tea break. He was nowhere to be seen in the attic, and the caretaker eventually tracked him down to his home. The plumber told how he was working away when he saw the figure of a woman in white. When she passed through a solid wall, the plumber had rushed off home, badly shaken by the experience.

The house had seen many tragedies in the past, so it would not be surprising if it were haunted. John Smith, having bought the house in 1801, lost his eldest son the same year when he hanged himself. Three years later he lost his youngest son, Charles, who died aged thirteen, followed one month later by the suicide of his daughter Mary at the age of twenty-four. She was soon to be married, but one day, first laying her wedding dress carefully on the bed, she hanged herself from the bedpost. Could she be the lady in white?

But death was to again visit the house later in the century when there was an outbreak of typhoid. At that time Joseph Thompson owned the house and had a forge on Boythorpe Road. In 1848 two of his daughters, Sarah and Jemima, died within three days of each other, followed by his only son, Frank, the following month. Only daughter Lydia escaped death, making a slow recovery from the dreadful disease.

The building eventually became a private club. Going about his tasks one day, the caretaker entered a room at the back of the stage in the main hall. His torch picked out the shape of a black cat with eyes blazing. With a snarl, the cat leapt over the terrified man's head and disappeared. The caretaker was so upset that it took all of the powers of persuasion his wife possessed to tempt him back to work the next day. There, talking to colleagues about his experience, he heard the story of an unfortunate cat. At a time when the building had been closed for two weeks, the cat had been mistakenly locked in a room. When the room was reopened, the dead body of the cat was found. It would not be surprising if the cat was still spitting-angry at the style of its death.

But the caretaker's house was not exactly an escape from strange events. It has been the location for strange smells, footsteps and hovering globes of blue light. Some local history has disappeared with the demolition of the house. It remains to be seen if the cat and the lady in white stay on to haunt future buildings, as some spirits are wont to do.

Rose Hill

Chesterfield Town Hall is a splendid red-brick building with a commanding position at the head of a steep slope. It was opened in 1938. The architects were the same as those for the Northern Ireland Parliament building, which it strongly resembles.

But it was not the first building to occupy that site. Around 1730 a fine house called 'Rose Hill' was built there. Even though it was very near to the town centre, the busy market place a mere few minutes walk away, it was the focus of a private 9-acre estate. At that time the occupants of the house had views over open land, some of which would become Queen's Park in Victorian times.

When the estate was about a hundred years old, Mr James Ashwell bought it. As with most large houses of the time, there was a full complement of servants who could be summoned by the pull of a bell rope. The servants knew where they were required as each bell rope activated a bell on a board, and the room name was written below each bell. Shortly after Mr Ashwell moved in, the bells began behaving in a very strange manner. They started to ring all by themselves, when no one had pulled a bell rope. Draughts were ruled out as the house was sturdily built of stone and brick faced. It was then thought that the servants might be responsible. Apparently the owner locked the servants in the library in order to try to establish if they were indeed the culprits. As the bells only rang daily from 5.00 a.m. until 11.00 p.m. and then sometimes ceased to ring for months on end, it is to be hoped that they were not kept imprisoned for too long!

Mr Ashwell established, to his satisfaction, that members of the staff were not to blame. Being a man with a scientific mind he decided to study the bells very closely. He found that when they rang by themselves, they swung to and fro in a regular pattern and then stopped suddenly. Had a rope activated a bell, it would have swung in an ever-decreasing arc until it came to a stop. Moreover, he noted that one bell always led off the 'phantom ringing', to be followed by a second, then a third and finally a fourth. He changed the position of the bells on the board,

Chesterfield Town Hall, built on the site of Rose Hill House, where servant bells rang mysteriously.

only to find that they continued to ring in their self-appointed order wherever they were placed. He even held on to one of the bells as it began to ring, so stopping it, but when he let go, it immediately began to ring again. Like-minded friends visited from as far away as London, but none could offer an explanation.

The house had, by now, acquired a reputation for being haunted. So it was with some trepidation that a workman approached 'Rose Hill' with his ladder and tools, having been employed by Mr Ashwell for one final drastic experiment. It had been decided to sever the bells' connections to their bell pulls. The workman set to work, cutting the wires to the bells. The household waited with bated breath. The bells again rang on their own!

Finally admitting defeat, Mr Ashwell called the workman to re-connect the bells. As he climbed the ladder to connect the first bell, it rather cheekily rang in his face. The workman descended the ladder extremely rapidly, leaving it and his tools behind.

The mystery of the bells was never solved, even though they went on misbehaving for eighteen months. The only comment about a possible cause was that they had begun to ring automatically on the arrival of a governess and ceased when she left. But no connection could be made. The ringing of bells by themselves was not unique to Chesterfield. Major Edward Moor wrote to an Ipswich paper in 1834 about the mysterious ringing bells at Great Bealing in Suffolk. A friend of Mr Ashwell wrote to him about the similar events at Rose Hill. Eventually Major Moor wrote a pamphlet listing nearly seventeen such phenomena.

Eventually the Borough Council bought the estate and demolished the house. The council moved into its newly built Town Hall in 1938, and nearly all that remains of Rose Hill is the name, which was given to the road which fronts the Town Hall. What also remains is the unsolved mystery of the bells.

Bank Close House is near to the town, but well secluded by trees. Who was the little girl seen here?

When a mischievous spirit causes mayhem in a building, such as the phantom bell ringer at Rose Hill, they may well transfer their 'presence' to the succeeding building on the site.

A councillor, his wife and a male friend were returning borrowed furniture to the Town Hall one Saturday evening after a fund-raising event. The door at the west end of the building had been left open for them. As they walked along the well-lit corridor, the wife remarked, 'That was a nice young man', turning as if to look at a figure. Her husband and his friend were startled by this remark and assured her that there had been no young man. She thought that they were teasing her, and was adamant that she had seen the figure of a man. He had not been a ghostly shape, as that would have frightened her, but an apparently solid figure. The two men were as sure there had been no man, as the woman was sure that there had. They never agreed.

Bank Close House

Just before Hasland Road swings right to join the bypass, there is a gateway on the left-hand side. A long curving drive leads to a fine gentleman's residence, well hidden by trees. Bank Close House is believed to have been built around 1830. Many of the windows retain wooden shutters. These, plus the elaborate plasterwork and wrought iron staircase banister, have earned this house a Grade II-listed status.

At the beginning of the 1850s, William Drabble, a solicitor, occupied Bank Close House. He became a very important man in the town, serving as mayor on four separate occasions, 1853, 1854, 1856 and lastly in 1861.

He lived in the house with his wife Elizabeth, his stepdaughter, Eliza Penelope Clay, and three servants. Eliza Penelope married a wealthy landowner from North Wingfield called Joseph Bright.

The driveway to Bank Close House. A coachman was murdered on this drive during an attempted robbery.

The Brights were paying a visit to Bank Close House in September 1868, from their home in Hathersage, when a dreadful tragedy occurred. During the evening noises were heard outside. John Holmes, butler to the household, and Joseph Bright armed themselves with sticks and went outside.

There they apprehended a man who had potatoes in his pockets, obviously dug up from the kitchen garden. George Kelk, the Bright's coachman, got involved as he was coming up the long drive. As there were people passing, having had an evening out together in Hasland, they became involved too. During this time it began to rain and the butler turned back to the house for an umbrella. As he did so, the thief, during a scuffle, stabbed George Kelk to death. The passers-by had been asked to help but as they were returning from the pub and not quite sober, they had been unable to prevent the tragedy. A single stab wound had severed the femoral artery at the top of the thigh, and death came quickly. The killer was eventually caught and sentenced to fifteen years imprisonment.

Poor George was buried in St Paul's churchyard, Hasland with the following headstone:

George Kelk of Old Coates, Notts, died 26 September 1868 aged 30 while in the discharge of his duties, met with a sudden and cruel death in the parish. The stone was erected by his late Master and Mistress of Nether Hall, Hathersage.

Tube Industries (TI), once located on the A61 near Horns Bridge, bought Bank Close House in 1946 and owned it until 1983. TI closed and was demolished and the Alma Leisure Complex now occupies the site.

Bank Close House is now a residential care home. Although there are plenty of people around the building nowadays, none of them was present nearby when the manager heard her name repeatedly being called. Could it have been that poor coachman who lies in the graveyard in Hasland so far from his native Nottinghamshire? And who is, or was, the little girl who was seen upstairs by one of the cleaners? So unnerved was she that a priest was brought in to bring peace to all concerned.

The tranquillity which now exists in and around this house belies its colourful past.

The much-extended Murray House is now the Municipal Golf Club, Tapton Park.

Murray House

Set high on rising land to the east of the town is the municipal golf club, Tapton Park. The clubhouse is based around a Victorian brick residence named Murray House. The original property has been extended to each side, but the double-fronted house is still obvious, as is the lodge at the end of the former drive and the stable block beyond.

Despite the tranquil green surroundings, the head groundsman and his staff were constantly aware of some sort of presence in the area. This was especially disturbing when they were on duty early at the weekends and had to unlock the buildings around 6.30 a.m. As they did this, they reported the feeling that someone was watching them, even though the only other living creatures about were rabbits. New members of staff also commented on this strange, frightening feeling.

About twenty years ago, the then assistant golf professional had a very unnerving experience. There was a room at the club that was used by the staff to repair members' golf clubs. One morning the man unlocked the door and entered the room only to find it in complete disorder. Clubs, which had been left for repair, woods and irons, were broken and scattered about on the floor. Storage racks had been tipped over and were lying face down. There was no evidence of the door having been forced open and it had definitely been locked, as the professional had had to open it with a key to enter. Horrified, he rang his supervisor. The members were reimbursed for their clubs and the affair was hushed up. The room also contained a fireplace. Many golfers reported seeing the ghostly figure of a man leaning over it. The fireplace has since been removed.

Golf repairs were later done in a small room in the old stable block. Formerly it had been a rest room for groundsmen and also had a fireplace in it. One day, a member of staff, entering the room alone, was terrified to see the almost transparent shape of a man, casually leaning on the mantlepiece. Unable to speak, he could only watch in horror as the ghostly figure faded away. But that was not the only strange event which occurred in that room. A member of staff decided to take his midday break there. As he sat peacefully reading, he heard the scraping noise of a bolt being drawn. He looked up, to see the bottom bolt on the door that led into the rest

The haunted stable block at Murray House that is now in a derelict state.

of the stable block moving on its own. When the top bolt also began to scrape and move on its own, the man made a hasty exit.

Several years ago a London contractor was called in to install a new sprinkler system for the greens. Most of the workforce slept in a caravan parked near the stables. They had to send for a company bricklayer, but there was no room in the caravan so he offered to sleep on a small settee in the small rest room. He had obviously not heard any of the stories of hauntings, being from outside the area, nor was he told any, or he might have thought twice about his offer! Locking himself in that evening, he was no doubt congratulating himself on securing a private little 'bedroom'. Next morning, however, he was found outside the building vowing never to enter it again. He had awoken suddenly during the night to find the figure of a man sitting looking at him.

Imagine his panic as he fumbled to unlock the door and escape the figure that appeared to need neither keys nor door to enter the (far from restful) rest room.

Tapton House

Nobody seems to know the exact date of the building of Tapton House. It is set on rising ground to the east of the town with wonderful views towards the parish church and beyond. The style of the lovely Grade II* listed building would suggest it was built in the late eighteenth century. The first occupants were the Wilkinson family, Isaac being an important banker in the town. Other famous occupants followed, including, from 1871 to 1925, members of the Markham family. They founded the engineering works that built, among other things, landing craft for D-Day in 1944 and some of the tunnelling machinery that was used to dig the Channel Tunnel. The Markham machinery lies under the Channel to this day, buried in the wall of one of the tunnels. The market for their heavy engineering goods was worldwide. Sadly the company is no more, and the works site has become a housing estate with all buildings demolished, with the exception of the office block.

HAUNTED CHESTERFIELD

The front of Tapton House, which George Stephenson occupied for the last ten years of his life. His ghost has been seen both in the house and the stable block.

Charles Paxton Markham gave Tapton House to the borough in 1925. His mother was the daughter of Joseph Paxton, hence his unusual middle name. Paxton came to Chatsworth House as head gardener in the early nineteenth century. He designed the Crystal Palace for the Great Exhibition of 1851. Tapton House is now part of the Chesterfield College Campus, but the grounds are open to the public. Around 1841 Robert Stephenson came to live in Tapton House. He so enjoyed his life there as a country gentleman that it seems he was reluctant to leave after his death.

For a short time in the late 1920s the house was unoccupied. This proved to be quite a temptation to a group of young schoolgirls who had vowed to visit the deserted mansion one day after school. But Margaret, one of the group, lost her nerve and refused to go with them. However, later she regretted her decision and decided to go alone one Saturday. Telling her parents that she was going to a netball match, and wearing her school uniform to make her story more believable, she set off up the hill. Although the garden was rather neglected she remembers that the daffodils were in bloom. Finding the stables she pushed open the old door to the coach house, and was delighted to find a coach there. Although it was rather dirty, she scrambled up on to the worn leather seat and sat there pretending to be a fine lady.

After a while, she began to feel very uncomfortable, as if she were being watched. Looking up, she saw a gentleman with a fine set of whiskers wearing a tall, black hat. She was not afraid and his demeanour was quite friendly, but she felt that she should not really be there, so she fled home. Alas, she could not keep her visit secret as her clothes were rather dusty, and she told her parents of her visit to Tapton House and her strange encounter.

It so happened that Margaret's father had once worked as a footman there and her description exactly matched that of George Stephenson. His ghost had been seen many times wandering around the house he loved so much. He may even have been pleased to see the young girl enjoying her imaginary ride in a carriage.

In 1931 the house became the first selective school in the Chesterfield area. More than 260 scholarship pupils attended classes in the beautifully proportioned and decorated rooms. Although most of the classrooms were numbered, one room bore the initials S.R., Stephenson's Room. This was the room in which he died in August 1848. It is to be wondered how many

Side view of Tapton House. The gardens, which Stephenson enjoyed so much, are open to the public.

Being a great innovator himself, George Stephenson might forgive the building of the Innovation Centre in his beloved walled garden.

of the pupils realised that they were sharing the building with the ghost of the great railway engineer, George Stephenson (who, incidentally, was illiterate until the age of eighteen).

The caretaker's wife was apparently unaware that she was sharing the building with his ghost until one day when she was sweeping a corridor. Steps at the end of the corridor led to a locked door. Suddenly, she heard a man's voice asking why his water had not been brought up! Startled, she looked up to see the figure of a man she did not recognise. She noted that he was dressed in rather old-fashioned clothing. The man repeated his question, apparently mistaking the woman for one of his servants who had failed in their morning duty. Mumbling an apology, the woman ran to get her husband, who was nearby. They returned to the corridor, but it was deserted. The 'man' had not come past them, nor would a real human being have been able to leave by the door at the end, for it was still locked.

The headmaster heard of this unnerving event and invited the woman to look at an album of portraits. One of them she immediately recognised as the man she had seen in the corridor. It was a portrait of George Stephenson.

George has not been seen around Tapton House for some time now, but the building is 'haunted' by former pupils of the selective school. Their interest is not in ghost stories, however, but in the magnificent cantilevered staircase. As it was reserved in the past for teachers and visitors, these elderly ex-pupils now delight in climbing the 'forbidden' stairs even though there is now a lift.

Lodge Farm

As you approach Junction 29 of the M1 on the southbound carriageway, the ruins of a farm are clearly visible, isolated in a field off the Palterton Road. They are quite 'romantic' and photogenic as ruined properties go, but the supernatural events that have occurred in and around Lodge Farm are far from romantic.

Nearly sixty years ago, in the winter of 1948, one of the farmer's sons returned from business in Carr Vale, near Bolsover. He retired to bed about midnight, with the light of a candle to show his way. He was exhausted and soon began to fall asleep, but he was rudely awoken by the sound of footsteps. Then, in the pitch-blackness, he felt a gentle touch on the forehead. Terrified, he fled downstairs, where he spent the rest of the night with the light of a paraffin lamp for comfort.

Footsteps were often heard padding around the interior of this isolated building. Although rats were used as an excuse for these sounds, it was not so. Whatever phenomenon was causing the disturbances seemed to be drawn towards the room where the farmer's daughters slept. In the silence of the night they sensed a presence other than their own, and they too heard footsteps apparently circling the bed. As the terrified girls lay rigid under the covers, one of them felt a light touch that had not come from any human sibling. These events continued night after night. In the end, the family became so intimidated that they refused to go upstairs, and the dog, with that uncanny sense of the paranormal which they seem to possess, lifted its head to the ceiling and howled.

An Italian prisoner of war once came to stay at the farm. Derbyshire, being a long way from the coast in either direction, was considered a safe place to have internment camps and often the prisoners were sent out to work in the surrounding area. He was given a bed in a front room, which had a barred window. He was found next morning in a great state of agitation, proclaiming that the room was haunted and begging to go back to the camp. Although the door to the room was solid, and the handle very stiff, some non-human hand had spent the entire night turning the handle, and opening and closing the door, until the poor man was nearly deranged with terror.

The deserted ruins of Lodge Farm. Terrified members of the family were forced to sleep downstairs.

The surroundings of the farm have also been the backdrop to a strange event. A relative was visiting the farm on a motorbike. He knew the area quite well and so decided to take the shorter route and cut through the fields. There were two gateways on this route. As he approached the first gatepost, he saw a man standing by it. It was rather strange as it was ten o'clock at night, but country people can keep late hours, and this man appeared to be dressed like a farmer. He had leather leggings and wore a raincoat and a bowler hat. The motorcyclist spoke to this fellow late-night traveller, but received no answer, nor did the figure show any sign of movement or turn his face towards the friendly greeting. Assuming that he must be deaf, the relative carried on to the next gate about 200 yards further on. To his astonishment there was again a figure standing at the gatepost. Could it be the same man? By the light of the motorcycle lamps, the rider checked carefully. Yes, it was definitely the same figure, wearing the same clothing. The 'farmer' could not possibly have covered the distance between the two gates quickly enough to arrive before the motorcyclist. The rider speedily turned around and took the long route to the farm, no doubt arriving a very shaken man.

Indeed, he must have been unnerved, because his return journey was made with a tractor following closely behind, its lights full on to show the road, and with a twelve-bore shotgun close at hand. Just in case…

But there is a story that may explain the presence of the figure at the gates. A tenant farmer who had previously occupied the farm had imprisoned a woman to prevent her seeing her man friend. One day the farmer went to market, but never returned. Perhaps he was murdered by the lover, and is spending eternity in futile attempts to return to the farm.

Home Sweet Home?

Haunting is not, of course, confined to public buildings. Many people experience supernatural events in their own environment, but very often these stories remain within the family. Fear of being unable to sell the house may inhibit storytelling, but there are those who wish to share their experiences, albeit anonymously.

One such woman tells of strange events in a house in Brampton. The children often heard laughing and giggling. A family friend heard the noises only once and declined to visit the house ever again. Both mother and children sensed the presence of a man and a woman, distinguishing them by their smell. The 'woman' smelled of perfume, while the 'man' smelled dirty and of cigarettes. Other events included drawing pins from a pin board being thrown against a radiator, each landing with a nerve-jangling 'ping' and something sitting on the end of a bed. There was a rumour that a former occupant had hanged himself on the landing.

The house had been a family home for a long time and grandfather had been nursed there until he died. One day the grown-up granddaughter heard him coughing upstairs. Without a second thought she rushed upstairs with a glass of water and briefly saw the figure of her grandfather lying in bed just as he used to do. He thanked her before disappearing. It is hardly surprising that the family dog refused to go upstairs considering their sensitivity to supernatural presences.

In another house, a family witnessed some very weird behaviour from their dog in a downstairs room. For a period of about a month the dog would not cross the centre of the living room, but would only walk close to the walls. Efforts were made to try to break this behaviour, such as carrying him to the centre and putting him down on the floor. On each occasion the dog fled to the side of the room. Later on the family learned of something that might explain the dog's behaviour. Some years before, a man had suddenly died in the room about that time of the year. He lay sprawled on the floor in the centre of the room until he was found. Was the dog avoiding the aura of the spirit revisiting the place of his death?

Again in Brampton, a young man had just retired to bed when he heard a loud knocking on his door. His friend was begging a bed for the night, having been locked out of his own home after a night out. Had he been doing the famous 'Brampton Mile' – that pub crawl from the long-gone Terminus near Storrs Road to the town centre, taking a drink in each of the fifteen or so pubs along the way? Whether or not he had, he was more than willing to sleep on the friend's settee.

He was awoken very early in the morning by the door to the room opening. Still half asleep, he asked his friend why he was up and was told that he was just going to attend to the fire. Later, at breakfast, the visitor was told that his friend had not got up to tend the fire. He had no need to, as it was a gas fire!

As his head cleared, the visitor recalled that the attentive figure had not resembled his friend but had been dressed in a long nightshirt, was smoking a cigarette and carrying a candle. Many of the houses in Brampton are Victorian terraces and this figure was obviously from a much earlier period in the history of the house.

The Brimington House

If any place in the area can claim to have the greatest number of supernatural events, it must be a house in Brimington which lies to the north-east of the town centre on the A619. It was built on the site of a former coach house that was demolished in the late 1960s. The couple that had the house built had known the former resident of the coach house. He was an elderly man who was most fastidious about the fireplaces in the building. Even when he was close to death, he got up from his sick bed to attend to the cleaning of the flue boxes.

There were no problems with the new house for three years. The husband then decided that it was time to sweep the chimneys. It was after this was done that all the strange and worrying events began. As will be seen, many, but not all, the phenomena seemed to have some connection with fire, and the conclusion was arrived at that the former owner was still around and keeping an eye on the place. The 'fire' phenomena even followed the woman to her place of work.

The first event was unexpected and shocking. The couple arrived home from work one day to a terrible mess. On the archway separating the two living areas were black hoof prints (remember, this site had been that of a former coach house) and on looking more closely they could see that the hoof marks were formed from soot. After the shock had worn off they set about cleaning the wall, and, with the help of a neighbour, erased the marks. But that was not to be the end of it. The hoof prints reappeared the next day, were cleaned off and reappeared the day after that. The cycle continued for several days until the cleaners won and the hoof prints, thankfully, did not return.

The couple may have thought that they could relax, but to their horror the next event also involved a mess and more cleaning up. As they prepared to leave for work one morning they went into the living room to find the windows covered by a black substance which again proved to be soot. It had even infiltrated between the panes of glass in the double glazing. The distraught wife was eventually calmed down enough to help her husband clean up. The double glazing was penetrated on another occasion, but this time by a white substance. It was also over the carpets, up the walls and in the hallway. The substance could not be collected for analysis, for when an attempt was made to scoop it up, it 'melted' away. Then it all disappeared as mysteriously as it had come.

Another event which was connected with fire involved the teenage daughter. On entering the bathroom she found it to be full of smoke, but there was no fire and, being a bathroom, there were no sockets to overheat. Moreover, the smoke stayed strictly within the confines of the bathroom walls and did not drift out through the open door, as 'normal' smoke would have done. It then disappeared. From time to time, the family smelled smoke round the house which they described as being like the smoke from a steam train, although there was no railway near the house, nor probably any steam trains left by that time.

The smoke phenomena followed the wife to work, to the consternation of the staff. When smoke began pouring out of a side room, there was a rush for exits and fire extinguishers. But there was no fire or electrical defect. The firm dealt with flip-top book matches. On examination, one new book full of matches was found to be useless. All the matches had been struck and yet there was no scorching on the packaging. Other books of matches in the box were checked and many were found to be in the same state; struck, spent but no scorching.

There is an old saying, 'There is no smoke without fire'. However, once the family literally experienced the opposite, 'fire' without smoke, for they found that they had constant hot water even though the immersion heater was switched off. This happy 'haunting' of the water tank carried on for six weeks, after which the free supply of hot water sadly ceased.

The family 'ghost' also had a mischievous, and sometimes destructive, side. The mother retired to bed one night leaving her husband and daughter watching television downstairs. When she felt her husband climb in beside her, she asked if the daughter were still downstairs. There was no reply and so she repeated the question. Again no reply to that question, or the third one.

Stretching out her hand to his side of the bed she was terrified to find it empty. She fled downstairs where both husband and daughter were still watching television. It was a very long time before she was persuaded to go back to bed.

The kitchen was also a place where tricks occurred. The family decided where they would like to keep the tea and sugar containers, but this did not suit the spirit. Every morning they would come downstairs to find they had been moved across the kitchen. This happened every night until the family decided to leave them where they found them in the morning, and their nocturnal wanderings ceased. The family would often come across jars and tins with all or maybe just some of the contents missing. They learned to leave them alone and eventually they would find them refilled. A neighbour was given a knife that had belonged to the wife's mother, but next day it reappeared in the kitchen drawer. Every time the knife was given away it returned of its own accord. This went on for four weeks until the knife was 'allowed' to stay.

The figure of a woman was seen in the kitchen one day. She faded away, but was seen long enough for a description to be given to a neighbour, who said she resembled a former occupant of the coach house, perhaps one who knew her own mind when it came to organising a kitchen!

As before, the phenomena also happened away from the house. The woman's boss kept a bottle of whisky in his office for entertaining customers and company representatives. One day he found the bottle empty. The staff professed to know nothing about it and laughingly accused the boss of being a secret drinker. When the woman arrived back home she found a full bottle of whisky in the fridge. Knowing by now to leave well alone, she did not touch it. Next morning it had gone and the boss's whisky bottle was found to be full again.

Friends, relatives and neighbours also witnessed many of the strange happenings. For example, during a coffee break with a friend the rubber plant bent into a complete U-shape, only to return to normal again before the friend had left. One day a woven straw bag was found to have disappeared, but in its place were two balls of straw, one cream and one brown, the two colours of the bag. Many friends saw the two balls of straw which, when left alone as the family had learned to do, rewove themselves back into the bag. After a social visit, a friend, having taken his shoes off for the evening, was unable to find the second shoe on leaving. Although the house was thoroughly searched, the shoe could not be found. The guest went home in his socks. The next morning the shoe was found – in the middle of the kitchen floor.

One rather expensive episode involved a bag of newly bought glassware. Although the bag had been carefully placed out of the way in a corner, the contents were later found to have been smashed to pieces.

Locking the doors of a house should be a simple task, but one evening this turned into a nightmare. The front door was locked and bolted, and the back door was being attended to, when the front door flew open. They ran to re-lock the front door only to hear the back door burst open again. There was to be half an hour of frantic running backwards and forwards between the doors until both were secured and the couple could retire, exhausted, to bed. What kind of spirit could have put the family through so much over the years?

Eventually they were persuaded to contact a Spiritualist Society. No conclusions were reached but the major haunting episodes dwindled. There was still the feeling of a 'presence' and cold spots from time to time, but the family had learned to co-exist with whatever, or whoever, had caused them so much distress over the years. Their fortitude can only bring on profound admiration.

CHAPTER FOUR

PLACES OF BUSINESS

The Old Registry

At the end of Union Walk, where it meets Newbold Road, is a fine red-brick building with an elaborate door case. This 1895 building was once the offices of the Guardians of the Poor, the local worthies who administered the nearby Union Workhouse. The building has also been, as its name suggests, the office of the registrar.

During its time as offices, many people have worked there. Some will never forget what they experienced. When the Social Services were based there, one man was known to stay late, night after night. This eventually ceased to be a matter for comment. But one day he left at the same time as all the others, and continued to do so. This did cause some comment. For a long time he would not say why he had changed his working practises. Finally he confessed and told his story. Whilst working late he had heard cleaners in the building, not unusual outside normal working hours. But on leaving his office he found, to his dismay, that although he had heard all the typical clattering, sloshing noises of a person cleaning the corridor, there was no one there! Fearful of being laughed at if he told his colleagues, he had kept quiet. When he eventually told of his experiences, he found that he was not alone; others had also heard the phantom cleaners.

One evening, a far-from-phantom cleaner was working as part of a team when she glanced into an office to see a woman hard at work. Not recognising her as a regular team member, she assumed that she was a new recruit. She did note that her clothes were rather old-fashioned, but decided that they must be just old work clothes. At the end of the shift, as they prepared to leave, she noticed that the woman was not with them. Enquiring if she should fetch the 'new lady', for she would have had to pass them to get to the exit, the supervisor replied that there was no new recruit to the team.

The present-day cleaning team report that they often hear noises in the cellar. It can only be surmised that the building is haunted by cleaners. Are they women who so enjoyed their work that they have returned to it after death, or is cleaning for eternity a dreadful punishment meted out to those who do little or no cleaning during their earthly life?

The front of the Old Registry with its ornate doorway, and date stone of 1895. Many people working late in the offices in this building heard cleaners, but could not see them!

The Tube Works

Chesterfield Tube Works occupied a large site at the end of Derby Road. After its closure and demolition, the Alma Leisure Park was built, which included a multiplex 'Cineworld' cinema.

The works had a security fence and gates with offices for the security guards who were on duty twenty-four hours a day. In the mid-1970s, after a guard had completed his first round of inspection, he locked himself in the office at the Number 6 gate and sat down to read the newspaper. He looked up briefly and was horrified to see a man just standing in the locked office. The figure did not move. The security guard stated that if it had, he would have dived straight through the window! The figure then faded away and the trembling guard pulled himself together enough to phone a colleague.

Early one morning a 'strange person' was seen waiting to enter the gate. But as the gates were opened, he faded away. The description of the man matched that of a deceased security guard, and his family believe he went back to work just to do one more round of duty before his eternal rest.

A figure was also seen many times by canteen workers. Now the site has been redeveloped, have the 'fading figures' of nearby Horns Bridge and the Tube Works taken up residence in the cinema?

Horns Bridge

As you approach Chesterfield from Junction 29, you will pass under a railway bridge. This is an important north/south link, operated by Midland Mainline. The modern line is the successor to the North Midland Railway, the building of which brought George Stephenson to the town in 1838. The original line went through Staveley and Rotherham, whereas the modern line goes straight to Sheffield. The first railway station opened in 1840.

But Chesterfield could, at one time, claim two more railway lines and two more stations. The Great Central Railway took over the more direct north/south route in 1879. It has long gone, but those travelling along the Chesterfield bypass to the east of the town are on its route, for the railway line has become a road. The third railway line was the Lancashire, Derbyshire & East Coast Railway, which came to Chesterfield in 1899. Sadly, it did not achieve the aims laid out in its title, for ultimately it ran only between Chesterfield and a junction near Lincoln.

These three railway lines at one time crossed each other on bridges. They then carried the lines across the road, which is now the bypass to Junction 29 of the M1. The great Horns Bridge gives its name to this area although it has long been demolished. The solid brick wall of the bridge has been the scene of strange sightings. Numerous people have seen the figure of a man disappearing through the wall. These have occurred both during the day and at night.

A workman returning home to Hasland from Bryan Donkin's Gas Valve Works saw a man crossing the road. To the workman's astonishment, he then walked straight through the wall. What also amazed him was that a man walking his dog, coming from the opposite direction, appeared to see nothing at all, for there was no reaction from either dog or master. They walked unconcerned past the very place where the figure had been seen to melt into the bricks. Dogs are thought to have special senses over and above those of human beings. Certainly the dogs that were taken down to the haunted cellar of the Sun Inn, and refused to enter, sensed something they were not prepared to face. The guard dog at the brewery also refused to enter the premises when the alarm was ringing. So why had this dog not reacted?

Even stranger, then, is the account given by a man of the opposite reaction of his dog. One day, during a walk which took them under the railway bridge, the dog ran off and would not heed any calls to heel even though it was normally obedient. It then ran straight into the wall, badly injuring its face in the process. Was the dog chasing a figure, like the one reported by so many people, which had then disappeared into the wall? Its sixth sense seems to have allowed it to see the figure and yet not be afraid of it. Sadly it could not stop in time, and suffered the consequences.

The busy roundabout at the end of the bypass to Junction 29 of the M1. Formerly three railway bridges crossed the road at this point, and a dog hurt his nose chasing a non-existent figure!

The front of the Yorkshire Bank, formerly a residence known as the Manor House, where 'horrible apparitions' were seen.

The Yorkshire Bank

The splendid gable-fronted property overlooking New Square has long been used as bank premises. It is currently the Yorkshire Bank. Originally it was a private house, re-fronted and rather grandly named 'The old Manor House'. It was never a manor house. It overlooked an open area known at one time as Swine's Green, which became the New Market in the 1820s.

During the time it was a residence, 200 years ago, several female members of the family reported disturbing sightings of what could only be described as spirits from another dimension. A woman described how her aunt, walking through the first-floor rooms, came across a small child. It was not a family member, and as far as she knew there were no children in the house. However, maternal instincts came to the fore, and she stooped to pick up the child, hoping, no doubt, to restore it to its parents. To her horror, her arms went right through the child, who promptly disappeared. So upset was she that on fleeing to the ground floor to the comfort of family members, she leapt from landing to landing, ignoring the seven steps in between!

The grandmother of the niece relating the story also had a dreadful experience whilst awaiting the return of her husband, a local doctor. As she sat in the dining room she heard a clanking of chains in the hall and a ghostly prisoner joined her in the room. With great, and surprising, presence of mind she fled the room, locking the door behind her. But this did not deter the phantom, as it promptly melted through the door into the hall where it disappeared. The sister of this lady also saw a gruesome ghost. As she was reading the bible at the time, she flung the book at the apparition as a kind of do-it-yourself exorcism, and it evaporated.

Strange happenings have not entirely ceased at the present bank. The dining room was for a time the manager's office. It is to the right of the central door as you face the building. The dark wooden panelling of the original dining room is still there. Several years ago there were always problems with the computer terminal in this room. There were no problems with the rest of this system, just that part of it in the room once visited by an unquiet spirit.

Cleaners in the bank often reported that the queue dividers, consisting of posts with retractable tapes between them, would often move, the tapes swaying gently, even though there was no draught and no one had bumped into them.

Most un-nerving of all, a night supervisor reported that even though the telephone receivers throughout the building had been switched to his receiver, so that all incoming calls would be diverted to him, telephones were heard to ring in other parts of the bank during the darkest, loneliest watches of the night.

Brampton Brewery

Chesterfield had many new industries in Victorian times, largely in the Brampton area to the west of the town. The most productive of these was brewing, which led to the drunken, riotous nature of the town in those times. No less than three breweries supplied the relatively small (300 acre) town, and by the second half of the nineteenth century there were sixty-seven hotels, inns and taverns and fifty-four beerhouses. During the 1880s, Harold Soames ran the Brampton Brewery. At the time he rented Stubbing Court, a lovely eighteenth-century hall in nearby

Wingerworth. His daughter, Olave, born at the hall in 1889, married Robert Baden-Powell, and become the first Chief Guide.

Brampton Brewery was on West Bars. It was a magnificent turreted building, a veritable brewing palace, which produced its own local beer known as Brampton Ale, the last batch of which was produced in 1955. After brewing ceased, the buildings were used for other small businesses before being demolished in 1984. The DIY store B&Q now occupies the site.

Supernatural sights and sounds abounded in parts of the old brewery buildings used by small firms. The ghost of an old man, wearing the traditional cloth cap and mackintosh, was frequently seen around one room in the basement. His sightings were often accompanied by the smell of cigarette smoke. One deliveryman came face to face with this figure, believed to be the ghost of a long-dead night watchman, when he was taking goods into the basement. Surprised by his appearance, the man asked who he was and what he was doing there. The figure vanished.

For a while, a clothing manufacturer used the building. One day, a manager told his supervisor that he was going out, but would be back by 6.00 p.m. She decided to wait for his return before locking up the building. The machinists had all gone home, so she was alone. She switched on the tannoy system, the better to hear when he returned. About 5.45 p.m. she heard heavy breathing over the system. At first she was not too frightened because she thought that her boss was playing a joke. Hoping to get her own back, she used another door to creep down to the main door and surprise him. But he was not there. Terrified, she fled the building.

As the woman was in charge of girls in the workforce, she did her best not to spread her fear, but the girls themselves were to have a petrifying and inexplicable experience of their own. As she was working, one of the girls glanced at the windows. There she saw human faces pressed against the glass, staring into the room. She screamed. Others looked up. They, too, saw the faces and screamed in unison. They all agreed that they were 'real' faces and not just imagined. What had really fuelled their fear was not only the faces at the windows, but that the room in which they were working was at least 40ft above ground level!

The ghosts were not just nosey – they were noisy. Footsteps and banging doors were heard constantly round the building. One evening, after the building had been locked up for the night, a passing taxi driver heard such loud noises that he thought the building was being burgled and vandalised. He called the police. They found no evidence of any forced entry and all the banging doors the man had heard were firmly locked.

There were many further examples of out-of-the-ordinary occurrences. A security guard, investigating the reason why a burglar alarm was sounding, found that his guard dog absolutely refused enter the premises. Two men walking across a yard found that they were bound, for at least a minute, by a force that would not let them continue. When a windscreen company occupied the buildings, the employees frequently reported feeling that they were about to be touched on the shoulder. They found that when they were trying to close doors to lock them, they encountered resistance.

But the ghosts were not the only ones who produced noise. A member of the Spiritualist church on the same site came to ask the girls to turn their music down as it was interfering with their attempts to contact the spirit world. As she left, she informed them that there was a presence in the building but that it was friendly. No doubt the girls who saw the faces at the windows were relieved to hear it!

CHAPTER FIVE

SHOPS NOW AND THEN

Former Freeman's Temperance Hotel

Corporation Street, in Chesterfield Town Centre, seems to have had more than its fair share of haunted buildings. To the Pomegranate and Hippodrome Theatres must be added the furniture warehouse, which took over the former hotel. Footsteps, cold spots and the opening and closing of doors were merely worrying phenomena compared with the activity in the bedding department. This proved to be rather a dangerous place to work. Whilst shop customers may have been concerned with the softness of their mattresses, the frightened warehousemen were more concerned with dodging them as they flew through the air!

But even this must have seemed less dangerous than passing through the stockroom, where the aim was to escape unscathed as beds came hurtling down on the unfortunate employees. The building was demolished in 1980 and one could not blame the former members of staff if they breathed a sigh of relief as they moved on to safer working environments.

Ford's Bookshop

The bookshop may be long gone, but the building of which it occupied a small part is still firmly in place. Chesterfield Market Hall was opened in 1857, after the Borough Council petitioned Parliament for permission to build a place for market traders to avoid the inclement weather. At that time the two-acre market site also accommodated live animal sales. The fine building contained an Assembly Room and a courthouse in addition to shops and stalls. It still dominates the centre of town to this day, with the very useful clock presented by the Duke of Devonshire ten years after the opening.

On its north side, under a stone-carved coat of arms, was Ford's Bookshop. The Children's Department was downstairs. One morning an assistant saw a man walking towards this department, almost as if he were intent on buying books for the family. But he was not of our era, for he was clothed in a frock coat with a high collar more in keeping with the Victorian period, when the building was new.

Left: *The mid-Victorian Market Hall stands proudly in the middle of the large Market Square in the centre of town.*

Below: *Ford's Bookshop was either side of the arch beneath the stone carving, on the north side of the Market Hall.*

Although the assistant was taken aback, her experience was not as frightening as that of a girl who also saw a figure, who walked straight across the shop and through a closed door! This ghostly encounter reminded her of how many of the staff felt uncomfortable when in the basement. It always seemed as if there had been a presence there. The atmosphere was chilly, that common indicator of a supernatural occupation, and whilst down there, many people reported feeling as if they were being watched. Perhaps the man in the frock coat was a former manager or a lost member of an audience seeking out a popular 'Penny Reading' in the Assembly Room above.

The premises of Stuart Bradley, jeweller, face down the new street called Steeple Gate. The window to the left of the door appears to be haunted.

Stuart Bradley – Jeweller

Stuart Bradley's jewellery and gift shop occupies one of the fine Victorian buildings still left on the north side of this street, which leads to the parish church. The business moved to the premises fairly recently and work was carried out to adapt the building to its new purpose. During the work a badly burned kitchen door was revealed, but no one seemed to know the cause of this fire or the results.

The members of staff were disconcerted to find strange things happening. In the jewellery repair workshop at the top of the building, tools, left in a specific order at the close of business, were found to have moved the next morning even though the door had been locked. In addition, objects began to fall off shelves in the window to the left of the door.

A shoe shop had originally occupied this part of the building. The former manageress reported that one morning, as she and a colleague arrived for work, they both saw a shoe hovering in that window inches above the shelf.

The staff at Bradley's now make sure that nothing breakable is displayed on a shelf in that particular window, just in case…

The Victoria Centre

On the north side of Knifesmithgate are black and white buildings, reminiscent of the Tudor period, which are now known collectively as the Victoria Centre. In fact these buildings were constructed in the 1920/30s, and are supposedly modelled on the Chester Rows. The elegant covered pavement, so useful in wet weather, sports wooden carvings that resemble gargoyles on Gothic churches. Behind this pseudo-architecture is a genuine architectural gem: a chapel built in 1694. Originally a Dissenters chapel, it is now Unitarian. Dissenters were those people who refused to accept the new Book of Common Prayer in 1662. They had to worship secretly until William and Mary came to the throne and brought in the Act of Toleration in 1689. The

The Victoria Centre on Knifesmithgate was inspired by the Chester Rows. Is it haunted by those who previously occupied the site?

The side of the Elder Yard chapel, built in 1694, as seen from Elder Way. The front of the chapel originally faced Knifesmithgate. The churchyard was cleared to build the Victoria Centre.

chapel was built to face onto Knifesmithgate with a graveyard around and in front of it. Over the years, other buildings were to crowd in on the seventeenth-century chapel, businesses such as foundries and rope-makers, and, in 1912, a billiard hall. Eventually the site was redeveloped with the buildings we see today. Although all retail units now, the complex once had a ballroom and an early cinema, the Victoria.

The graveyard and some old industrial units were cleared for the construction of the Victoria Centre buildings. Some have claimed that not all the graves were emptied and that might account for some of the mystifying events experienced by occupants of the centre over the years: taps and lights turned on and off, locked doors left open and footsteps heard. A group of men narrowly missed being hit by a piece of wood hurtling downstairs towards them. On investigation, there was no one above them who could have thrown it. Many people reported the feeling that they were not alone, as if they were being watched, but on turning round, found that there was no one there. Such was the feeling of terror in one part of the complex that many staff dreaded going in there, saying that apart from the sensation of being watched, they felt a cold atmosphere as well as feeling clammy. Work in that area, the old projection room of the Victoria cinema, was completed very quickly! A dramatic turn of events convinced the staff that there was definitely an unwelcome presence in the room.

At that time the room was being used to store sink tops, and a young man was sent in there to count them. A short while later he came rushing out on to the main retail floor apparently terrified, and claiming that someone was messing about. When the distraught young man was eventually calmed, he told them that first the temperature in the room dropped and then he had felt what he could only describe as arms circle his body from behind. As the grip from these 'arms' grew tighter and tighter, they appeared to grow hotter and hotter in contrast to the chilly room. Finally his terror gave him the strength to break free. He went home ill, but never returned to work there.

But perhaps it was not an unquiet spirit from the graveyard. Oliver's Foundry formerly occupied that site. The company had been founded in the 1850s and did so much heavy engineering work that the company grew too big for the site and relocated to the Broad Oaks Meadows to the east of town alongside the river Rother. The company was eventually sold on and became Markham & Co. (This highly regarded company has now closed, but its legacy remains in the many tunnels which were constructed using Markham Tunnelling machinery such as the London and Moscow undergrounds and the Channel Tunnel, where the Markham tunnelling machinery remains, embedded in the wall. Colliery winding gear, water turbines and tunnel shields were also manufactured. The office building remains on the road to Bolsover but the site has now been developed as a housing estate.

A dreadful accident at Oliver's Foundry, when it was on the Knifesmithgate site, may well be the cause of the young man's terrifying experience in the projection room. Ropes were attached to pulleys for lifting heavy goods. The apprentices were warned to keep clear of the ropes, as becoming tangled in them could be disastrous. One young apprentice either failed to heed the warning, or was just unlucky, as a rope became wrapped around his waist. Counterbalanced by the weight on the other end, he was dragged up to the roof. When they got him down, his waist was much reduced in measurement. The ever-tightening rope had squeezed the last breath from his lungs.

The coils must have felt like arms gripping him and friction must have made them grow hotter and hotter. Had the man in the projection room felt the replication of that terrible event? Was the apprentice trying to make others feel what he had suffered? Perhaps his terror had been transferred to those who entered the room.

CHAPTER SIX

THEATRES AND CINEMAS

The Pomegranate Theatre

George Stephenson, the great railway engineer, came to live in Chesterfield in 1838 to oversee the building of the Midland Railway line between Derby and Leeds. In semi-retirement by then, he moved into Tapton House to the east of the town and devoted part of his time to the pursuit of growing exotic plants such as pineapples, melons and grapes. He enjoyed being in competition with the 6th Duke of Devonshire's gardener at Chatsworth House, one Joseph Paxton.

Stephenson died in 1848 and is buried beneath the floor of the chancel in Holy Trinity church, which lies between Newbold Road and Sheffield Road.

Stephenson was so highly regarded in the town that a building was erected in his honour using money raised by public subscription. Stephenson's Memorial Hall was built in less than two years and opened in the summer of 1879. The great hall of the building, which also contained science laboratories, classrooms and a library, was to become a cinema and then, in 1949, the first civic theatre in the country. It was renamed the Pomegranate in 1982.

Stephenson's ghost is said to haunt both Tapton House and the theatre. What nicer places could you have to spend your eternity than a splendid country house and a lively theatre? The ghost of a stagehand who committed suicide in more recent times could have joined him, as well as an actor who died in the theatre.

Whoever it was, an actress saw a figure when she was standing on the stage with a producer. The indistinct form was looking down from the upper circle, an area in which others had said they sensed 'someone' breathing down their neck. While the woman could see the figure, the man could not. But he could see the door opening and then closing when the woman described it leaving the circle by that exit. Had that figure also turned the page of a script being held by a producer as he briefly looked away?

During a break in rehearsals, an amateur group retired to a room off the stage to enjoy a Chinese takeaway and a few beers. They were then astounded, and not a little disconcerted, to hear a tune being played on a piano, which was on the deserted stage! It was not an electric piano or harmonium but a perfectly ordinary piano that needed some pressure on the keys to make it play.

But mischief and scare tactics aside, a ghost certainly enjoys being a patron of the theatre. One evening, an employee counted the admittedly rather thin audience and reported to a colleague

The Stephenson Memorial Hall at the head of Corporation Street houses the town's museum and the civic theatre called the Pomegranate.

The Pomegranate Theatre on Corporation Street is part of the George Stephenson Memorial building. Is George the ghost who occasionally occupies a seat in the stalls?

that there was an extra seat occupied. The female colleague came to count the members of the audience, and found the number *did* tally with that of the ticket sales. But the man was adamant that there was an extra person, in Victorian clothes, enjoying the performance – for free.

The Hippodrome

Corporation Street was built in 1870 as an access road to the Midland railway station. When the inner relief road was built in the early 1980s, Corporation Street became a cul-de-sac, with only a footbridge linking this part of the town to the Chesterfield Hotel and the station. In 1896 a theatre was built on the opposite side of the street to the hall which was to become the current theatre. It was sited just above the hotel. The original name was the Theatre Royal but in 1912 it became the Hippodrome. It was a popular variety act venue, and in 1908 began showing that new and exciting entertainment – films.

The theatre hosted pantomimes and, in 1925, a company which was starting rehearsals for the show *Rip Van Winkle* advertised for local girls to audition as dancers. The custom of using local dance talent for pantomimes continues to the present day. A fourteen-year-old girl who went to Greenham's School of Dancing on Beetwell Street was delighted to be accepted after she had attended auditions. Late one afternoon, after school, she made her way to the theatre for her first rehearsal. She waited at the door where she had been told she would be met. It was growing dark and the lamp was out. No one came to fetch her so she gently pushed open the door, apprehensive and excited all at the same time, and found herself in a dark corridor. Feeling her way along she was comforted, but apparently not frightened, to feel an arm round her shoulders guiding her along. Chatting about how grateful she was for the help and how thrilled she was to be taking part in a professional show, she seemed not to notice that her 'companion' was silent.

The door at the end of the corridor opened on to a brightly lit stage. The actors, looking towards the opening door, were surprised to see the girl turning to thank thin air! When she told them of her experience they informed her that she might have met a ghost. Later she found a dressing room locked and was told that an actor had died there and people would not enter it any more.

Was it the actor's ghost, or was it the ghost of a member of a double act in the old days of variety who died on stage thirty years before the young dancer's experience? He was a widower whose three children travelled with him. Two of the children went to relatives in Manchester but sadly they could not take the third, who was blind. He remained in a school in Chesterfield and thrived, marrying and producing descendants who wonder if the friendly ghost at the Hippodrome was their relative.

The theatre closed in 1955 and has since been demolished.

The Palace Cinema and Woolworths

The Woolworths store on Burlington Street, not far from the Crooked Spire, was a popular and busy shop, but there were customers and staff who were never happy with the atmosphere at the back of the store. Not always able to identify what the feeling was, they just felt that it was 'not right'. A saleslady told of the practice of taking a colleague into one of the storerooms because staff disliked going there alone.

A Saturday girl remembers that when she was asked to weight out loose nails in order to bag them, she found that they felt warm, not cold as she might have expected from metal in a storeroom. When the cellar floor needed re-surfacing, a workman was asked in to do the job. At the end of the day he smoothed the concrete over, left his tools neatly lined up and left, locking the door behind him. On returning the next day, he unlocked the door and was amazed to see that his tools were in disarray. Also, there was a footprint firmly embedded in the now set concrete floor.

But the strangest thing to occur in this building was the smell of smoke – without fire. Those who smelt it also reported hearing screaming and crying. A fire had occurred many years before, a fact which was unknown to some of those who reported the distressing sounds and smell.

The store had been built on the site of a former cinema called the Palace, where one of the greatest tragedies in the town's history had occurred. On 27 December 1911, several young girls in their early teens were waiting excitedly in a small room in an adjoining building owned by the cinema management, ready to appear on stage in a concert. Amongst them were twelve-year-old Lydia Smith, who was a pupil at the school in Vicar Lane, and Elizabeth 'Lizzie' Bell, who was thirteen and already working at Robinson's pillbox factory in the town. She had had special permission to leave early to be in the show. Films in those days were only several minutes long as opposed to several hours nowadays, and the young dancers had been trained to make the Christmas shows special occasions by having live performers in addition to the new and wondrous moving films. They had already performed on the previous night to great acclaim.

There were several different costumes among the dancers, including Eskimo costumes made of cotton wool which would prove to be a fatal choice. There was a fire in the room, with an efficient fireguard and an adult supervising the children. Despite these precautions one of the girl's Eskimo costumes caught fire. It flared up instantly and panic followed. Poor Lizzie was this first victim. In agony she rushed around the small dressing room setting fire to the costumes of other children before rushing down the stairs in the passage below, where passers-by extinguished the flames. Her father came running from his nearby home (many more people lived in the town centre in those days). The badly burned child, with her blackened face and ruined costume, was leaning against the wall. Mr Bell asked her name. Only when she replied faintly did he realise that it was his own child. She whispered, 'Take me to mummy'. Wrapping her in his coat and one loaned from another man, he rushed her to hospital.

Meanwhile, Mrs Elliott, the chaperone, tried to put out the flames, receiving severe burns, as did many of the children trying to help their panic-stricken friends. Ada Tidsall had gallantly tried to put out the flames on her friend Lizzie's costume, burning her own hands and setting her own costume alight. Mr Taylor, the manager, calmed the audience who had sensed the pandemonium around them. Members of the hospital staff were having their own Christmas entertainment, but this was put aside to treat the injured. Despite their best efforts, five of the children died; Lydia (twelve), Lizzie (thirteen), and Ada (thirteen), together with Winifred Wood (fourteen) and Mabel Swain (thirteen). The children were buried in Spital Cemetery, to the east of the town, on 1 January 1912.

The Palace cinema was later demolished, and Woolworths was built on the site. And so began the strange events which echo the great tragedy of nearly a century ago.

The Cineworld multiplex cinema on Derby Road, on the site of the former Tube Industries Ltd. T.I. works were haunted and so is Cineworld.

Cineworld

Having been without a cinema for a while, and forced to drive to Crystal Peaks near Sheffield to see a film, people in Chesterfield were pleased to see the opening of a Cineworld multiplex in 1998. The former site of Tube Industries Ltd and the Alma public house became a busy leisure park. The factory and the pub may now be distant memories, but do the ghosts of TI and nearby Horns Bridge still haunt the area? Many staff at the cinema think so.

The projection room seems to be the main focus of events. With many screens in the same building, the projection room is long and narrow with projectors to each side throwing their images onto the screens through small portholes. A window at the side allows the projectionist to view the film on screen. The wide films are wound on huge reels set horizontally, which are called 'platters'.

One of the present managers sensed a presence in the room and now refuses to go up there. Another was attending to a platter when he felt the urge to keep glancing up to a particular corner because he was sure there was someone looking at him. He thought it was the projectionist, but Karen was elsewhere. She has heard her name called three times in a woman's voice, and it wasn't a duty manager! A figure has definitely been seen but most of the sightings are of a reflection in the glass of the viewing portholes. People see a reflection and assume that someone is walking quietly behind them, but not so. It is not likely to be other members of staff, because few care to visit this long, dimly-lit room, for fear of seeing images that are not on celluloid.

CHAPTER SEVEN

FOUR GRAND HALLS AND A CASTLE

Hasland Old Hall

Today, you would look in vain for Hasland Old Hall, which stood at the corner of Calow Lane and Chapel Street. It was demolished in 1984 and garages were built on the site, and then town houses, which occupy the location now. But the hall lives on in photographs and memories. Unfortunately, not all the memories are happy.

Although the date of the building of the hall is not known exactly, it could be early fifteenth century, as John Linacre, who died in 1488, once occupied it. To Cestrefeldians (natives of Chesterfield) the name Linacre brings to mind the lovely walks around the three now redundant reservoirs to the west of the borough. These supplied the town with its drinking water during the Victorian period. The name Linacre comes from the family of that name who held a manor in the area. John is less well known than his brother Thomas, who was a great scholar. He qualified in medicine in Italy and at Oxford, where he also taught. There is a plaque in Old Brampton church recording that he was also the 'Initiator and First President of the Royal College of Physicians'.

Other occupants of the hall over the years have included Captain Roger Molineux and Captain John Lowe of Alderwasley. Captain Molineux defended Bolsover Castle in 1644 during the Civil War. The owner, the 1st Duke of Newcastle, was a great Royalist who only ten years earlier had welcomed Charles I and Queen Henrietta-Maria to a banquet and masque at Bolsover.

After these grand occupants, the hall apparently became a coaching inn with stabling and well for refreshment of the horses. Then, in the twentieth century, the venerable old hall was split into three parts for family occupancy. However, some of the previous residents of the hall do not appear to have entirely moved on.

Over fifty years ago, a woman lived in one part of the hall with her six children, five daughters and a son. They became quite used to the diminutive figure of a woman who walked about the rooms. They were not even too amazed when she apparently walked up the wall, for they knew that she was treading on the steps of a staircase that had been ripped out long ago. A white rabbit was also seen about the building. Whilst the small lady, and rabbit, seemed harmless, the daughters were very frightened by a spirit that dragged the bedclothes off their beds. This was terrifying enough, but they all then felt a chilly hand stroking them across their faces!

These town houses on Calow Lane, Hasland, are on the site of Hasland Old Hall. Before its demolition it was home to a variety of phenomena, including a lady who climbed up the wall.

But it was the mother who was to have the strangest experience of all, and feelings that led to her saving her son from almost certain death. The woman felt melancholy all day and could not shake off the feeling that something was about to happen. The feeling was so strong that in the end she could not deny it: she took her sleeping son from his bed and slipped him in beside one of his sisters. During the night a whole section of the hall collapsed, and a beam of wood from the ceiling smashed down on to the bed where her son had been sleeping not long before. It would be good to think that the friendly little lady, who walked on the non-existent stairs, had given the mother a timely warning.

Hagge Hall

Sir Peter Frecheville built the sixteenth-century Hagge Hall in Staveley as a dower house or hunting lodge. The Frecheville family acquired the estate through marriage. The previous owner, Nicholas Musard, died around 1300. He was a Catholic priest and so, of course, did not have an heir, although he did in fact have children! The estate passed to his three sisters, one of whom married Anker de Frecheville, Baron of Crich. The Frecheville family had come over with William the Conqueror, as had the Musards. By the mid-1540s, the whole of the Staveley estate was in the hands of the Frechevilles. Sir Peter was also responsible for building Staveley Hall in 1604. Later that century the Devonshire family took over the estate. Staveley Town Council now uses the hall as offices.

Hall Lane, leading to Hagge Hall, was the scene of an attempted elopement by the youngest daughter of Sir John Frecheville. Frances, born in 1638, was enamoured with one Colonel Thomas Culpepper. They crept from the hall at night and together they drove down the pitch-black lane. Sadly, the coach met with an accident which spoilt their plans. However, later on the two did marry, although still against the wishes of Sir John. He certainly would not have approved of his daughter marrying a man who became involved in a brawl with the Earl of

The tiny chantry building on the High Street in Staveley, connected with historic local families.

The plaque on the chantry. The Frecheville family lived at Hagge Hall and a member of the family has been known to haunt it.

Devonshire at the court of James II! Father eventually had his revenge on her for her wilfulness by cutting her out of his will. Frances did not have a happy life and this could be why she haunts the lane and hall. Many people have seen her at night in Hall Lane, the very time of her doomed elopement plans. She wears a cloak and hat; no doubt still trying to conceal her identity from her angry father.

In Hagge Hall itself, now a private house, she is often seen as a white lady. One Irish gentleman, a guest in the house, encountered the lady on the stairs as he went down to breakfast. He enquired of his host if the lady would be joining them for dinner, to be told that this was hardly likely as she was 300 years old!

Hagge Hall, now Hagge Farm, has been haunted by a white lady as well as having a 'haunted' tree in the garden.

An old rhyme, quoted in Arthur Court's book about Staveley (1946) tells of the haunting:

Then as you cross the entrance hall to ascend the oaken stair
Fear not to meet the lady who oft-times lingers there.
In cloak and hat of antique guise and robes of purest white,
She vanishes from the gazer's eyes, e'er in the noontide light.

The grounds of Hagge Hall also hosted a supernatural phenomenon, but this time it was not a ghost, but an ancient oak, known as the Haunted Oak. On it grew, in great profusion, the parasitic mistletoe, not normally found to grow on oaks in Derbyshire. When it was damaged, the tree oozed red sap instead of clear. This was disconcertingly similar to blood, as if the tree were actually wounded and bleeding. It also gave a half-human shriek when damaged, so it is not hard to see how it acquired the nickname 'the Mandrake Tree'. In mythology, the mandrake was said to have forked roots like two human legs, and to shriek when pulled out of the ground. A narcotic could be made from its roots.

The tree was fenced round with timber and later by earth banks. This was because an eerie voice, emanating from the tree, had prophesied that the hall would fall down if the tree were cut by human hand. Despite all efforts to shore up the tree, it was damaged and finally fell. Fortunately the tree was not demolished by human hand, but by a storm on 12 December 1883, and so Hagge Hall was safe.

The shell of the once magnificent stately home Sutton Scarsdale Hall can be seen from the M1 by people travelling south.

Sutton Scarsdale Hall

Many who travel south along the M1 towards Junction 29, the exit for Chesterfield, cannot help but be intrigued by the massive building on the hillside to the west. Even without windows and roof, this Grade I listed eighteenth-century ruin is impressive. It is Sutton Scarsdale Hall.

The building was commissioned at the beginning of the eighteenth century for Sir Nicholas Leake, the last Earl of Scarsdale. But it was not the first house on the estate, for the history of the manor goes back many centuries. The first house was probably built in the early thirteenth century. The Leake's inherited the estate through marriage and the first member of the family to live at Sutton was Sir John Leake in 1489. The house was brought up-to-date in 1594.

Sir Francis Leake was made a baronet in 1611 and his son, another Francis, was raised to the peerage in 1624, becoming the first Lord Deincourt (the name perhaps coming from d'Eyncourt). Lord Deincourt was eventually given the title of the 1st Earl of Scarsdale by the king (Scarsdale was an Old Norse name meaning Skarfe's Valley).

The 4th Earl of Scarsdale employed the services of Francis Smith of Warwick, who also worked on Derby Cathedral, to design a grand house for him, and building began in 1724. And 'grand' it was. It was to become the finest eighteenth-century house in Derbyshire. The interior boasted fine plasterwork and carved marble fireplaces; columns decorated the outer walls and a balustrade ran all around the roofline. There were formal gardens and a landscaped park. Unfortunately Sir Nicholas never married, so on his death, in 1736, the hall had to be sold off to pay the debts incurred by building costs.

So began a chain of ownership, which nearly resulted in the complete loss of this fine architectural gem. The first buyer was Godfrey Clarke of Somersall Hall, who was a wealthy merchant. For the next hundred years the hall passed through many hands until 1824, when Robert Arkwright, the eldest grandson of Sir Richard Arkwright of Willersley Castle, Cromford, bought it. Robert's son sold the house in 1920, together with the 5,000-acre park, wisely retaining the mineral rights. The sale nearly resulted in the loss of the hall, because a speculator bought it, and slowly began dismantling it. When the roof was removed, some of the fine interiors went to a museum in Philadelphia, USA. So slow was the process that the main walls were still standing when Sir Osbert Sitwell, of Renishaw Hall, came forward in the 1950s to purchase the remains to save them. It is rumoured that the deal went through on the final day before demolition!

If Sir Osbert and the family had plans to renovate the hall, they never came to fruition, and, in 1969, the Department of the Environment was called in to begin preservation, which has carried on under English Heritage. No fleeting glimpse from the motorway can reveal the fascinating history of this manor, nor can it hint at the legend and stories surrounding it.

During the medieval period one Sir Nicholas Leake was involved in the Crusades in the Middle East. On leaving his home, one of the former residences on the manor of Sutton Scarsdale, to travel on yet another Crusade, he vowed to his wife that he would return as quickly as possible. Taking off his wedding band, he cut it into two halves, giving one half to his wife, and keeping the other. Unfortunately the Turks took him captive during a battle. Throughout his many years of captivity he prayed for his safe return home. He vowed that if he were granted his wish, he would provide for the poor of his parish.

After falling asleep one night, Sir Nicholas awoke to find himself on the doorstep of the church near his home. Desperate to see his wife and family, he staggered to the house, only to find that the servants did not recognise him and sent him away, thinking he was an impostor. Eventually he remembered the half ring he had kept for so many years. He persuaded a servant to send it to his wife, who, recognising the love token, rushed to greet her long-lost husband.

True to his word, Sir Nicholas provided for the poor of the parish and, in his will, commanded that this charity should continue. So each St Nicholas Day (6 December) seven bushels of wheat were baked into loaves and given to the poor of the parishes of Sutton, Temple Normanton and Duckmanton. This tradition carried on until the death of the last Sir Nicholas Leake, the builder of Sutton Scarsdale Hall, who died in 1736.

It is not surprising that people describe an eerie atmosphere around the hall. Apart from being a ruin, it is next to a churchyard. Nevertheless, dog walkers pass the hall regularly and have described hovering coloured lights. A professor from Nottingham and a friend saw what they thought were ghosts with no legs. They were in white and appeared to be wearing hoods with slits for eyes. These shapes were attributed to white owls, but what explains the smell of tobacco smoke and phantom footsteps?

Workmen from the Department of the Environment had strange experiences while making the ruins of Sutton Scarsdale Hall safe.

Many men working to stabilise the building have described strange happenings, especially in the cellar. One labourer working on his own in the cellar heard footsteps cross the ceiling and then 'clump' down the stairs. He was meant to be alone on the site, so who could it be? Bravely, he flung open the door at the bottom of the steps, but there was no one there.

There was a stove in the cellar as it was cold work up on the windy ridge overlooking the Vale of Scarsdale. As the workmen gathered round the stove to warm themselves, they all heard voices coming from behind the door at the bottom of the steps. Again, when they opened the door, the stairs were deserted. The men were not the only creatures on the site. Taking pity on a cat one cold day they kindly carried it down to the cellar, thinking it would be grateful for the warmth. Far from it! The cat was normally a very placid, friendly animal, but on reaching the cellar the cat flew into a frenzied rage, scratching wildly in order to escape. It tore up the steps and was not seen for many hours. Something undetectable by humans had terrified the poor thing.

Similarly, a dog must have detected something strange when being taken for a walk across the churchyard. Suddenly the hairs on its back stood on end; it looked at the door to the hall and then ran, sniffing, to the door of the church. Surely it could not have detected the returning crusader in his filthy prison clothes? Could it?

Above left: *Traces of the plasterwork remain inside the ruins of Sutton Scarsdale Hall, showing what a splendid place it was. It was set to be the Chatsworth of East Derbyshire.*

Above right: *What was it in the cellar of Sutton Scarsdale Hall that terrified both the workmen sheltering there and a cat they took down to warm up?*

Hardwick Old Hall, which Bess of Hardwick bought from her brother. English Heritage now takes care of the ruin of this once splendid hall.

Bess of Hardwick commissioned Robert Smythson to design her new hall. She was by then Countess of Shrewsbury, hence the letters ES on the roof of the hall.

Hardwick Hall

High on a ridge of limestone above the Vale of Scarsdale, to the east of the M1, are two great halls. Hardwick New Hall with its great turrets and many windowed walls overshadows the ruined Old Hall close by. The great carved initials (ES) and coronet of a countess on the roofline left no one in doubt that this building was the work of Elizabeth, Countess of Shrewsbury.

Bess of Hardwick, as she is more familiarly known, although few may have dared to call her that to her face, was born into the Hardwick family in the early 1520s. Her father, who farmed a small, 400-acre estate, died in 1528 leaving a widow, one son and four daughters.

From these comparatively poor beginnings, Bess was to become one of the richest women in England after the Queen Elizabeth I. Bess met her first husband whilst she was living away from home with richer relatives. This was a common practice to give the children a wider education. Robert Barlow, probably a cousin, was in ill health; Bess nursed him and they fell in love and married. Poor Robert died before the marriage was consummated, 'for they were of tender years'. He left her an annual income of around £66.

Little is known of Bess until her second marriage at Bradgate House, Leicestershire. She may well have been living there. Bradgate was the home of the family of Lady Jane Grey, the ill-used nine-day Queen. Sir William Cavendish was a rich widower with estates all over England. He had been a Commissioner for the Dissolution of the monasteries under Henry VIII. Although married barely eleven years, Bess produced eight children, six of whom survived, three boys and three girls. This was the founding of the Cavendish Dynasty. During their marriage William was persuaded to sell his other estates, and to buy the Chatsworth Estate in the heart of Derbyshire. The purchase was completed on 31 December 1549 – in both their names.

Sir William Loe was to be the third of Bess's four husbands. The marriage was short, but the widower had money to send his stepsons to Eton, and provide dowries for the girls. His wealth also allowed Bess to indulge her passion for building houses.

Bess then married George Talbot, 6th Earl of Shrewsbury, at Sheffield Cathedral in 1568. His second son (destined to become the 7th Earl) married Bess's youngest daughter, Mary, and Henry, Bess's heir, married the earl's eldest daughter, Grace.

The new Countess continued to spend a great deal of time on her building at Chatsworth. The great Elizabethan Chatsworth that she had built does not exist any more, as the present house was built on the same site around 1700. Only a wooden spiral staircase, which can be seen through a trapdoor on the roof, remains of the first Chatsworth. This building mania, coupled with the strain that the Earl endured when he was given the task of imprisoning Mary, Queen of Scots, led to a breakdown in the marriage.

In 1583 Bess bought the Old Hall from her brother, who was deeply in debt from the rebuilding of the family home. Bess received an income from her husband and later acquired more wealth following his death in 1590. She had spent much on the Old Hall but decided to build a New Hall nearby, employing the talents of Robert Smythson. Symmetry and light were Smythson's trademark, hence the wonderful windows and six towering turrets at Hardwick Hall. Bess lived in the Old Hall until the New Hall was finished in the 1590s. By then she was a very old lady, but she was able to enjoy her triumphant building until she died in 1608.

The Cavendish family went on to become not only the Dukes of Devonshire, but the Dukes of Portland and Newcastle as well. The main seat of the Devonshires was Chatsworth, but they owned and used Hardwick too. The Old Hall had continued to be used for overflow and staff accommodation until it was allowed to become a ruin in the eighteenth century.

The widow of the 9th Duke used the New Hall as a Dower House until death duties forced it to be sold. The National Trust took over the property in 1956. The Old Hall is in the hands of English Heritage.

Bess of Hardwick returned some 350 years after her death to startle a housekeeper, who was most graciously thanked for the great care taken of the house and belongings over the years. But it was a more mischievous spirit who played a trick on another member of staff in the New Hall. She was ironing in the Flower Room, taking care to fold the finished garments neatly. Another member of staff called her away for some help. On returning she found that the neatly iron clothes had been thrown on the floor, and had to be ironed all over again. A ghostly white cat seems to favour the Needlework Room; perhaps in life it kept the ladies company as they sewed.

Maybe the Countess keeps an eye on the visitors who come to the house, for many of them have reported a feeling of being watched in the Blue Bedroom. One steward reports that many visitors immediately comment on the chill feel of the room and some have even refused to enter it at all. A member of a paranormal society saw a grey lady there. Other bedrooms are 'visited' on the upper floors, for impressions of a body have been seen on beds as if someone (thing) has rested for a while. A blue lady frequently flits around both halls. Another female steward asked to be relieved of duty in the Great Hall, the first room entered by visitors. She frequently saw the figure of a young woman in Elizabethan dress. Could it be the ghost of Bess's troublesome granddaughter, Arabella, who had a claim to the throne and for a while was kept a virtual prisoner in the hall?

The thousand acres of park and woodland around Hardwick Hall is a scene of great tranquillity these days, but it was not so during the Second World War. The 1st Parachute Brigade occupied the park in 1941 and subsequently it became the depot and School of Airborne Forces. Every paratrooper who took part in the D-Day landings on 6 June 1944 had trained at Hardwick. In the 1970s, when Miller's Pond was drained, 600 bicycles were found in the mud. They had been 'borrowed' by troops when they missed their transport home after a night out! One sentry on duty at the South Gate challenged a stranger coming towards him. There was no reply and as the figure continued to come towards him, the soldier was forced to use his bayonet. But the figure, in neck ruff and plumed hat, was undeterred, and continued on his way. The guard had raised the alarm when the figure first appeared and refused to answer the challenge, so there were many witnesses to the failed bayonet thrust, and the strange apparel of the 'man'. A group of paratroopers saw a figure similarly attired when they were near Hardstoft. He was calmly sitting on a fence, watching them as they marched by. Then, as the men stared, he slowly melted away.

The figure of a man haunts the Old Hall and gardens and is also seen on the path beneath the walls of the Old Hall. Could this be Thomas Hobbes, the great English philosopher? He was born in Malmesbury, Wiltshire, in 1588, and educated at Oxford. Invited to be a tutor to the Cavendish family, he travelled widely with the 2nd and 3rd earls, both in Europe and in the county of Derbyshire. He published a work on the 'Seven Wonders of the Peak', possibly one of the first guide books to the region. His happiest times were spent with the Cavendishes. One of the things he liked to do was to walk up and down the hill at Hardwick until he had worked up a sweat: he would then pay the servants to 'rub him'. He said this would help him to live longer, and this exercise, coupled with giving up meat and alcohol, seemed to work, for he lived to be ninety-one! Is he still walking up and down the hill?

He is buried in the parish church of St John the Baptist, Ault Hucknall.

The memorial to the members of the parachute regiments who trained in Hardwick Park. Some soldiers had supernatural experiences during their stay.

Thomas Hobbes, the philosopher, enjoyed walking beneath the walls of the Old Hall when he was alive, and has been seen walking there long after his death.

Bolsover Castle dominates the skyline as you approach Bolsover. The Little Castle is on the left, the ruined state apartments on the right.

Bolsover Castle

After William I had conquered England in 1066, he rewarded the knights who had helped him by giving them large tracts of land. One William Peveril did rather well in Derbyshire. He received land in Castleton, where Peveril Castle was named after him, and in the Bakewell area, where Haddon Hall was established. He also aquired land on the ridge of magnesium limestone to the east of Chesterfield. In the latter area, at the beginning of the twelfth century, Bolsover Castle came into being, but not in the form that we know it today. It is still said in the county that William Peveril was the illegitimate son of William the Conqueror, which may well account for the generous allocation of land!

Bess of Hardwick's third son, Charles, rented the castle from his brother-in-law, Gilbert, the 7th Earl of Shrewsbury. In the early years of the seventeenth century, Charles bought the estate and began to build the Little Castle. Sadly, he was not to see its completion, but his son William took up the challenge enthusiastically, and so the fine castle, which can be seen for miles along the Vale of Scarsdale, and from the M1, took shape. It was, in effect, a 'pleasure palace' with richly decorated ceilings and walls that have been restored to their full glory by English Heritage. The Elysium Room depicts Greek and Roman gods and goddesses, whilst the Star Chamber has gold stars on a heavenly blue background. In the surrounding garden, the Venus Fountain, with its four Brussels lookalike manikin statues, plus the little trysting rooms set within the enclosing wall, give a clue to the activities that took place around this jewel of a building.

Right: *The grand entrance to the Little Castle. This seventeenth-century building was a place of entertainment, but it may hold a dark secret.*

Below: *The bake ovens just off the main kitchen in the Little Castle. A visitor saw something here that she described as 'evil'.*

Sir William also engaged the services of the Elizabethan architect Robert Smythson, and his son Huntington, as his grandmother had done at Hardwick Hall. Sir William was a keen and expert horseman and he had an indoor riding school and associated building constructed. They still exist today. State Rooms, now sadly ruined, were set along the ridge, with magnificent views from the windows and the terrace. King Charles I and his Queen, Henrietta-Maria, visited Bolsover Castle on 30 July 1634, when a wonderful banquet, including roast swans and bitterns, was served. Ben Johnson wrote a masque called *Loves Welcome to Bolsover*, to be performed on this very special, and expensive, occasion. William was to become the first Duke of Newcastle.

Sadly, during the Civil War he was on the losing side in the battle of Marston Moor, and had to flee Cromwell's forces. He spent fourteen years in exile, during which he wrote a book on horsemanship. After the war, Bolsover Castle was partly destroyed so that it could not be garrisoned ever again. For a while, in Victorian times, the little castle served as the local vicarage, for it was self-contained, having its own kitchen. What must the incumbent, and his wife, have thought of the lively wall paintings? Very little, for a whitewash brush was employed to cover some of them up!

Thankfully the castle now exists in (nearly all) its former glory. But those who enjoyed these lovely surroundings in the past may not have entirely left: so many visitors report seeing vague shapes and apparent supernatural apparitions that their experiences are recorded in a book. Bolsover Castle, now administered by English Heritage, has enough ghosts for regular ghost walks to be conducted around it.

One visitor had such a shocking experience in the Little Castle that she could only describe it as evil. It is a most disturbing and horrifying story. The woman was in the kitchens close to where the baking ovens are located. Suddenly, she saw a young woman crossing the room towards the ovens. She looked terrified and nervously glanced over her shoulder as if in fear of being discovered. She was carrying a bundle. When she reached to open one of the oven doors, the visitor saw that there were glowing coals inside. At that moment, to her extreme distress, she heard the screams of a baby. Her instinct caused her to step towards the young woman to avert some terrible crime. As she did so, all the visions faded away. What had she witnessed? Was it an echo of some dreadful event in the past necessitated by a less tolerant society? It is perhaps the most distressing of all the ghost stories in the area.

CHAPTER EIGHT

PUBLIC HOUSES

Somerset House

The present-day public house known as Somerset House lies just beyond the new Chesterfield Royal Hospital on the boundary of Calow village. It was formerly the farmhouse of a wealthy gentleman farmer. In 1934 it was the scene of a tragedy that was to have repercussions on the staff and landlords who later took over the building when it became a pub.

The farmer and his friends had been out shooting. Afterwards they returned to the farmhouse for refreshments. The children of the farm labourer, who lived in the adjacent cottage, came across the guns, which the hunting party had left unattended. A ten-year-old boy picked up a gun and began to play with it. He pointed the gun at his seven-year-old sister. It was loaded, and went off: the girl, fatally wounded, was carried home and died in her mother's arms. She is buried in St Peter's churchyard, Calow.

Since that dreadful accident, many customers have seen the figure of a small girl around the public house. Her description always matches that of the victim. So clear was her image on one occasion that a man thought it was his own daughter before remembering that she was safely tucked up in bed at home.

Many times, the staff found doors locked and bolted when they should have been open. When the lights in the cellar stopped working, an electrician was called in as the staff could find no simple answer, such as a blown fuse. The electrician could find no reason either, nor did he seem able to fix them, and yet half an hour later they were found to be working perfectly. One day, brass pigs fell from a shelf. This type of thing can be caused by vibration or an accidental knock, but why was it that the pigs fell from the shelf when the row of bottles in front of them stayed firmly in place?

Fifty years after the shooting there were still more strange happenings. The barmaid and the landlord both heard their names being called, but no other members of staff or family had called them. Overnight, the barmaid acquired scratches on her arms. She would not have been able to cause these herself, as she was a self-confessed nail biter and so had very short nails. The landlord then reported similar scratches on his back.

In 1990 the landlord's five-year-old grandson came to visit. As he and his family lived in London, and the accident was so long ago, he probably had not been made aware of the tragedy. Yet when he woke up to go to the bathroom during the night, he saw the figure of a girl. He had been unafraid, merely enquiring in the morning what the little girl was doing in the house. He

Somerset House was once a farmhouse where a tragic shooting accident took place.

must have thought it was another small visitor. It transpired that he had seen her in a doorway, and then she had disappeared at his second glance.

The landlords also say that they have never felt any fear at her presence. They wonder, as the years pass, if she will cease to haunt the place that was her happy childhood home – at least for seven years.

Revolution House

There is a distinct 'village' feel as you enter Old Whittington with its fine church and inns. In fact, the parishes of Old and New Whittington, together with Whittington Moor, only joined the borough of Chesterfield in 1920.

The large public house nearest the church, called the Cock and Magpie, quite overshadows its former self, for in front of the pub is the thatched cottage which was once part of the alehouse known as the Cock and Pynot, pynot being an old dialect word for a magpie. Both these birds now appear on the Chesterfield coat of arms. Originally a farmhouse, the old building is thought to date from the early seventeenth century and is now Grade II* listed. It was much larger in the past, and had its own brew house and stables. Its current name is Revolution House, which gives a clue to its importance.

The seventeenth century was a time of fierce religious debate, to say the least. James II followed his brother Charles II to the throne in 1683. He was a Catholic convert. With the birth of an heir by his Catholic second wife, Mary of Modena, and his repeal of the anti-Catholic laws, it was feared that he would turn the monarchy and country once more towards Rome. Politicians murmured subversively that his daughter, Mary, by his first wife, married to Dutchman William of Orange, should be given the throne, for they were Protestants.

Plots were hatched to bring this about. William Cavendish, the 4th Earl of Devonshire, met up with Thomas Osborne, Earl of Danby, and John D'Arcy. The Earl of Danby was a powerful man who had controlled Parliament at one time. He and Cavendish had been sworn enemies as a result of political intrigues, but they met to reconcile their differences in the face of King James' policies. Other groups met in York and Nottingham. Chester, too, may have been involved.

Revolution House is the remains of a once larger alehouse in Whittington, then called the Cock and Pynot. It played a part in the Glorious Revolution of 1688, hence its current name.

Revolution House is dwarfed by the new 'alehouse' behind. The tiny museum is haunted by a dog and a child.

The plan was for William of Orange to land in the north and, protected by forces under the noble lords, travel to London to overthrow the king. To allay suspicion, the three men posed as a hunting party, and met on Whittington Moor. But the weather turned bad, the rains came and the 'hunting party' took refuge in the Cock and Pynot in Whittington. There, huddled together in the space that became known as the Plotting Parlour, now demolished, they made their peace with each other.

In the event, William landed in the south. James II offered only token resistance and fled to France, leaving his daughter and her husband to take the throne and return the monarchy to the Protestant faith, as indeed it has remained to this day. The revolution of 1688 became known as the Glorious Revolution and was virtually bloodless. In 1694 the Earl of Devonshire was rewarded with a dukedom for his support, and Thomas Osborne became Duke of Leeds. John D'Arcy is not mentioned, so it is assumed that he must have died.

Revolution House remained as an alehouse for a further century before becoming a dwelling for a succession of tenants. Two hundred years after the Revolution, the Cock and Pynot alehouse was in a poor state of repair, but thankfully part of it was restored. Trustees looked after the building until it was transferred to the Borough Council in 1938. It is now part of the Chesterfield Museum, and furnished with local authentic seventeenth-century wooden furniture. Pewter mugs on the table give the visitor a feeling of stepping back into a local alehouse during the dangerous times of great religious conflict. In the corner of the cosy room is a replica of the 'plotting chair'. The original is at Hardwick Hall.

Many people who have worked at Revolution House say that they have sensed a presence in the building. Some have even seen a face peering in through the window. However, they say that they feel no fear and that the old building retains a calm and welcoming atmosphere. One person, looking out of the window one day, felt a tugging at the back of her cardigan as if a small child were demanding attention. Not remembering where she was, she automatically responded as a mother would, telling the 'child' she would attend to it shortly. Then, coming back to reality quickly, she turned round realising that she was in an ancient alehouse, and that she was alone. Although she tried to replicate the feeling of the tug, thinking that her cardigan may have got caught up in her skirt waistband or had 'snagged' on something, she could not.

The revolution was over 300 years ago but one possible member of the hunting party may still haunt the plotting room, for a dog has often been seen there. Perhaps he remembers it as a safe refuge from the inclement weather in north-east Derbyshire? Or is he just one of the many dogs who must have accompanied their masters to the cosy refuge in Whittington?

The Sun Inn

A few metres west from the New Market, which is to the rear of the Market Hall, is the Sun Inn. The current building, dating from 1912, has an imposing white tiled frontage with splendid brown ceramic 'swags' featuring pomegranates. (A pomegranate features on the town's coat of arms and is the name of the civic theatre.)

The original Sun Inn was a much plainer stone building with a traditional stone-flagged roof. A picture of the previous building is engraved on three of the windows. Although that building has gone, the original brick-vaulted cellar remains, as does the former coach yard where the stables housed fresh horses for coaches' on-going journeys. But one evening, as the horses were being well cared for, and the no-doubt chilly passengers warmed and fed, nobody thought about the coachman. When the time came to leave, he was nowhere to be found: he had been murdered and his body pushed down the 80ft well in the cellar. And so began the strange events in the cellar of the Sun Inn.

A publican who was taking over the premises moved in before his family and slept there alone for a few nights. But strange noises made him swear that he would never stay there alone again. On hearing music coming from downstairs he hurried to see if the jukebox had been left on. But no, the sound came from the cellar and moreover, the cellar door, which he had locked before retiring, was now open. Although noises continued to come from the cellar, they ceased to be 'musical' – in fact, far from it. One evening, loud crashes, again behind the locked door, sent the publican rushing downstairs to the cellar, where he found that stacked crates were in disarray all over the floor. They had been piled neatly against the walls and it appeared that they had been thrown about rather than merely toppled over. This occurred again and, in addition, footsteps were heard circling a slot, which is all that remains of the round entrance to the well.

The parlour of Revolution House is furnished with authentic seventeenth-century furniture, but the 'Plotting Chair' is a replica.

The Sun Inn. The cellars are still those of the original building: why do dogs refuse to go down there?

Three of the windows of the ninety-year-old Sun Inn are engraved with a picture of the original building.

The publican's wife refused to enter the cellar, as did their Alsatian dog. When it was taken downstairs, it planted all fours paws firmly at the door and refused to go in. Suspicious that this may just have been a nervous dog, many other people brought their canine pets along, only to find that none of them would enter the cellar. Dogs are said to have a sixth sense and it could be that all of them sensed a presence in the cellar that was not wholly human.

Other publicans followed the family with the dog and they too experienced bizarre events in the cellar. During the 1980s, the landlord was mystified one evening when the pumps on the bar failed to deliver the beer. He went to unlock the cellar door, which is in the public bar area and therefore always meticulously locked to prevent confused patrons falling down the steps. He inspected the plastic pipes which were attached to the top of the beer barrels, and which should have carried the beer to the bar when the pumps were pulled. He was astounded to find that the flow valves had been turned off. These are very stiff and it is often difficult for a flesh and bone hand to move them. No one had gone down to the cellar between the beer flowing normally and then stopping. If it were indeed a ghostly hand, then it was a very strong one. Even more recently the coolers in the cellar were switched off. As to do this is ruinous to the beer, staff would not have done such a thing. It would appear that the poor, murdered coachman is trying to draw attention to himself.

If we attribute the strange happenings in the cellar to the murdered coachman then who is, or was, the woman who has been sighted many times in the rest of the building? There appears to be no record of a woman being murdered, but then again, ghosts are also said to return to the place where they were happiest or still have work to do.

The Royal Oak

To the east of the main market place is a collection of intersecting streets known as the Shambles. As in York, the name denoted an area of abattoirs and butcher's shops. It is a corruption of the word 'Fleshamols', which were the wide windowsills on which the butchers displayed their meat. In Victorian times the area was well populated, many people living in accommodation above shops accessed by narrow staircases. What a stinking area it must have been with the blood of slaughtered animals running down the sloping streets! But the blood that was let in the Shambles was not always that of animals.

One Sunday night, 7 December 1845, the occupants of the Shambles heard what they described as 'murderous noises' coming from behind the door of a butcher's shop adjacent to the Royal Oak public house. One witness, Thomas Harvey, shoemaker, who was passing the shop around 7.30 p.m., described hearing three or four 'tremendous blows' followed by groaning and noises of suffocation. He fetched his wife to witness the sounds. People hammered on the shop door, but the man who was managing the shop at the time, Jack Platts, refused to open it. He called out that he had made the noises, as he had been sick following the drinking of a brandy. Later he was seen to have a cut on his hand, but explained this away as an injury from a broken lantern. Having heard these explanations, and assuring themselves that his girlfriend was safely in church, the residents of the Shambles returned to their homes. For this action they were later to be criticised at a murder inquest.

One evening, on 28 August 1846, Robert Ashley and Valentine Wall set about their unenviable job as night-soil workers. They had to dig out the contents of the pits under the wooden seats in the privies down the many long, narrow yards of the town. Thomas Green had the job of conveying the smelly mess to Hasland on his 'honey cart', where it was spread on the fields.

Above left: *The Royal Oak in the Shambles just off Chesterfield's Market Place. A dreadful murder took place in this area in Victorian times.*

Above right: *This building was once the Falcon Inn. It has a narrow yard down the side, one of many which used to exist in the town.*

Below: *In a Falcon Yard privy, the night-soil men made a gruesome discovery.*

The plaque on the Royal Oak in the Shambles. The area was known for its butcher's shops.

The three men were astounded when bones, with rotting flesh on them, began appearing from the privy in Falcon Yard, formerly Bunting's Yard. At first they thought they were sheep bones, but the eventual appearance of clothing convinced them otherwise. The black coat and trousers, canary-coloured waistcoat, side-laced boots and neckerchief with the initials G.C. identified the victim as George Collis, a young man in his mid-twenties. He had gone into partnership with the rascally Platts. His former employer had given the clothes to him when she had closed up her house, and had had to terminate his employment. When Collis's hat was recovered, it was damaged in a way that matched the damage on the skull, no doubt caused by the 'tremendous blows' heard by the witness on that fateful evening nine months before.

The inquest was held at the Shoulder of Mutton public house in Hasland on 3 September. The newspaper item in the *Derby Mercury* reported that the coroner's inquest 'sat on the remains', as, indeed, had many others!

Witnesses came forward to say that on 7 December last they had seen Jack Platts and accomplices carrying a five-foot bundle across the street from the Shambles to the yard opposite, Bunting's Yard. Collis's girlfriend, Ellen Beresford, reported having met with George on that Sunday evening when he had told her that he was going to ask Platts for wages he was owed, so he could go to Manchester the next morning to look for work. Ellen, who was pregnant with his child, saw him consult his watch at 6.35 p.m. before he left. The watch was later found in the possession of Platt's family. Nobody had missed the poor young victim as they thought he was in Manchester looking for work, and perhaps trying to avoid his family responsibilities.

Jack Platts was arrested and tried for murder. He was hanged in Derby on 1 April 1847, still protesting his innocence. He did request that he be hanged in the morning so that the people of Chesterfield would not be able to travel by train to witness his execution. But this request was denied, and, thanks to Mr Stephenson's railway, many were able to witness justice being done.

The Royal Oak public house on the corner of Iron Gate in the Shambles has the look of a fine medieval building. It is undoubtedly on the site of an earlier building, and the sign outside suggests this was a resting place for the Knights Templar, based at Temple Normanton. Records show that it has been an inn since 1722, which makes it the oldest inn in Chesterfield. It was

One of the bars at the Royal Oak was once a butcher's shop. Is this where a murder took place?

rebuilt at the end of the nineteenth century using many ancient timbers within its structure. The cosy lounge bar could almost be a small chapel, with timbers soaring to the full height of the roof and large leaded windows shedding light all around.

But it is the second bar that connects with the story of the dreadful murder in the Shambles, for it was once the infamous butcher's shop. There is still a butcher's block in the cellar. Around this area can be sensed a strange atmosphere. A psychic who came to the lounge bar saw the faint figure of a man standing there, wearing a black hat and coat. She thought it might be a physician, but it could have been poor George Collis in his new clothes. Perhaps it was the man known to have committed suicide in the building. The manager, Josh Clarke, and his members of staff, say that they frequently have the feeling that they are being stared at. There is a cold corner of the lounge bar where people do not like to sit. Although there once was a doorway there, it is bricked up and so cannot be causing a draught. Perhaps it is a drop in temperature signalling a supernatural presence.

Butchers vacated the Shambles over a hundred years ago in favour of the Market Hall, but the memory of the worst butchery of all lingers on in the narrow streets.

The Gardeners Arms (now The Gardeners)

The present building occupied by The Gardeners was built in 1927 for the Chesterfield Brewery Co., but there had been a public house on the site for a long time. Nor is a name change new, for the older, smaller building on the site was originally called The Grape. It was near a blacksmith's yard at the top of Glumangate. No doubt the blacksmith, and his visitors, found the inn a pleasant relief from the thirst-making heat of the forge. In 1862, another gentleman gave in to the temptations of the grape, in both senses, and slipped in for a drink. Unfortunately, he was a policeman on duty! He was subsequently dismissed from the force. The Grape became the Gardeners Arms in 1870.

HAUNTED CHESTERFIELD

The Gardeners on ancient Glumangate has been the scene of many strange happenings.

This public house is about half way up the unusually named Glumangate. Most of the buildings in the street are Victorian, but the name is medieval and probably unique amongst street names in the country. It is thought to be a corruption of 'gleeman', a minstrel who would wander from town to town entertaining with songs and no doubt spreading gossip and news. Such a person could have told of puzzling happenings at the Gardeners Arms.

There are only two entrances to the cellar of the public house; one outside to allow the draymen to deliver beer, and the other behind the bar. Although normally kept locked, one evening the door was open and the light on. The young man working behind the bar that evening was suddenly aware of a figure moving across the floor of the cellar. Amazed that anyone could have slipped behind the bar and gone down the cellar steps without anyone noticing, the young man, Jamie, quickly ran downstairs to check in case a customer had got lost. Despite the young man's conviction that the figure was solid and human, the cellar was deserted. Who, or what, had been seen was certainly not of this world.

Only last year Janet, who cleans at the Gardener's, saw a fleeting figure. She was vacuuming the carpet in the bar and had gone as far across the room as the cable would allow. She switched the vacuum cleaner off, and went to the socket to unplug it. Before she could do that, the vacuum cleaner started up on its own. Puzzled, she went to switch it off, and as she did so she glimpsed the shadow of a figure dart behind the bar. No other members of staff were there at the time. She carried on with her original task of changing sockets, but this time she took the vacuum cleaner with her, just in case!

But the spirits that appear to exist at the Gardeners mostly prefer the upstairs living accommodation to a cold and draughty cellar or a deserted bar. More than once, loud noises have been heard coming from upstairs. One former manager heard such a lot of commotion that she rushed angrily upstairs to admonish her children, whom she assumed were the cause. She was disconcerted to find that they were fast asleep!

Dawn, the current manager, has had exactly the same experience. She frequently hears running footsteps along the corridor, and taps in the bathroom have been turned on and left to run. In two of the bedrooms, which are unoccupied, the windows have been found to be open when they were left shut.

One New Year's Eve, when the bars of this busy, town centre pub were very crowded and noisy, there was such a racket on the first floor that the people in the bar heard it over their own merriment and several people ran to the bottom of the stairs only to hear 'shshshshing' noises like children make when they do not want adults to hear. The noise stopped. The upstairs was deserted at the time.

Another story of the Gardener's Arms tells of the figure of an old man in a certain chair in the corner of a bar who is only seen by an outgoing manager. The story is true. It has happened.

The Crispin Inn

The Crispin Inn, just outside the Eastern gate to the churchyard, has been part of the history of Ashover for many centuries. The name has two connections, one national, and one local. The national connection is with that famous St Crispin's Day (25 October) 1415, when the forces of Henry V met with those of the French on the battlefield now known as Agincourt. Although vastly outnumbered, Henry's forces triumphed thanks to the skill of the English longbow men. It has long been known that bowmen from Ashover were present at the battle. In common with many places, Ashover has a Butts road, 'butts' being the areas where medieval men were compelled to practice archery to hone their skills for the day when they were needed. Thomas Babington, a member of a local family, was there and he returned safely. What better way to commemorate the victory than to give the name of the saint's day, on which it was won, to the local inn, where no doubt the survivors toasted their luck and recounted their stories? The local connection is the Wall family, who ran the hostelry for many years and were shoemakers as well as publicans. There was also a cobbler's shop on the site. St Crispin is the patron saint of cobblers, harness and saddle makers.

Later, another war was to disturb the peace in Ashover, the Civil War. Derbyshire was under parliamentary law and Job Wall, publican at the Crispin Inn, was a supporter of Cromwell. When the king's troops came to the inn demanding drink, he refused them saying they were drunk enough already. They locked him out and drank the building dry. The rector at the time, Immanuel Bourne, lived at Eastwood Hall. Cavaliers took over his residence and their behaviour is recorded in one of his letters:

> They lived at free quarters and there was great slaughtering of pigs, sheep and fowles. They also did drink all the wine and ale in the cellars and then, drunken and madd, they did come down to the town and did the same in the alehouses. Job Wall withstood them in the doorway…

About the eventual destruction of the hall he wrote: 'It has almost broke my heart'.

A phantom cavalier has been seen near the ruins of the hall and horseshoes of the period of the Civil War have been found. Where once the horse-drawn coaches drew up in front of the inn, now there are many cars bringing visitors to this popular public house. Recent refurbishment seems to have disturbed a ghostly gang, for workmen reported feeling themselves pushed by unseen forces (as Job Wall had been pushed?). Many guests have reported feeling a chilly atmosphere in the place, a sure sign of spirits. The music in the bar once blared out very loudly even though the volume knob had not been touched – at least not by a human hand. One landlord, thinking a child was holding him by the legs, found that there was no one there. With such a lively history, is it any wonder that the Crispin Inn has many ghosts?

This House probably dates from the Year 1416 when THOMAS BABINGTON of DETHICK and several men of ASHER returned from the BATTLE of AGINCOURT which was fought on St. CRISPIN'S DAY.

In 1646 JOB WALL the Landlord of the INN withstood the Kings Troops in the doorway and told them that they should have no more drink in his house as they had had too much already.

But they turned him out and set watch at the door till all the ale was drunk or wasted.

The above incident occurred during the period when the Troops of KING CHARLES 1st were opposing OLIVER CROMWELL'S ARMY.

The Black Swan

This public house is a short walk away from the Crispin Inn. It is over 300 years old. Bear baiting was one of the entertainments offered in a large hollow nearby, but this 'sport' was coming to an end, for in 1810 John Smith was imprisoned for being a 'vagabond in charge of a bear'. When the television series *Peak Practice* changed locations from Fritchley, near Crich, to Ashover, the outside of the Black Swan featured strongly. The 'market' was set up just outside, but the interiors were shot elsewhere, including a bedroom in a house in Holloway! If the actors had used the first floor of the inn, they might have received a surprise, because the ghost of a woman has frequently been seen there. She walks along serenely before disappearing through a wall.

There is also the ghost of a laughing cavalier, who may well have moved in because of the overcrowding at the Crispin.

Right: *The Black Swan in Ashover also has its share of ghosts.*

Below: *The fifteenth-century Blue Bell Inn, North Wingfield, where a blue lady frequently visits.*

Opposite above: *The much-haunted Crispin Inn in Ashover, where the landlord turned away drunken soldiers during the Civil War.*

Opposite below: *The board on the wall of the Crispin Inn that tells some of its history.*

The Blue Bell Inn

Although now a public house, the Blue Bell at North Wingfield was originally a chantry house dating back to 1488. Monks lived there before the Reformation. There were also plans for a chantry chapel in the church. Chantries were usually built with money from a benefactor, who expected special prayers to be said for his soul.

In 1536, Henry VIII argued with the Pope over his divorce and ordered the dissolution of the monasteries. The Savage family then bought the chantry house premises. They continued to occupy them for several generations. Many members of the family are buried in the adjacent churchyard of St Lawrence's, where the mad monk roams.

The ghost of a Blue Lady haunts the Blue Bell Inn. She makes brief appearances both in the public lounge and the living accommodation. She is a rather dramatic female though, who likes to warn of her coming by playing with the lighting, making it dim and flicker before appearing suddenly from a blue haze. Also, prior to her visitation, bottles and glasses disappear and reappear, and once a bottle was struck from a landlord's hand to smash on the floor.

But friendly and lively as she is it appears that she does not like the cold, for she only deigns to appear in warm weather. Small wonder that she shuns the chilly churchyard – not to mention the company of the mad monk who haunts there.

The current licensee had not heard of the ghosts of the inn, but she quickly confirmed that she had indeed seen the figure of a woman in the entrance area and one side of the bar. 'What was she like?' was the question. 'Blue', was the answer! Moreover, she had seen a dog in the ancient beamed bar. It was a shorthaired black mongrel and was so realistic that she got on her hands and knees under the chairs and tables to look for it, but it had disappeared. One of the small shelves to the side of the bar is no longer used for the storage of glasses, because frequently they flew off the shelf onto the floor. Luckily the bottles now stored there have stayed put.

But perhaps most unnerving of all is the sensation experienced by the licensee: she has felt hands placed on her waist from behind, much as people feel when someone who is a friend squeezes passed in a small space.

But there is never anyone there. At least not from this dimension.

The Rutland Arms (Now the Rutland)

Tucked away behind the parish church is the public house previously known as the Rutland Arms. (The Earls and Dukes of Rutland have long held land in the county, Haddon Hall, Bakewell, being their main residence for many centuries, until they de-camped to Belvoir Castle, in Leicestershire, at the beginning of the eighteenth century. The premises now consist of two parts, the red brick property with a central door, and the white-stuccoed building to the left of it. A third building, the old hotel, was demolished in 1906 when Stephenson's Place was built.

During Victorian times there occurred a shocking tragedy at the inn. A young woman called Hannah Owen, aged only twenty, went to work there in 1875 as a cook and waitress. She had previously worked at the Old Angel Inn near the Market Place. When Hannah collapsed one day Mrs Boot, the landlady, thought at first that she had been taken ill with some sort of fit, but she quickly discovered that Hannah's problem was a fondness for drink, so she was dismissed. However, Hannah seemed to do so well at her new place of employment, the Rutland Arms, that she was held in high regard. But any problems she may have had with drink had not really gone away.

One Sunday evening, 18 July 1875, she joined with her friend, Ann Hibbert, for what was to be a walk around the town but ended up as the equivalent of a Victorian 'pub crawl'. A young man called Ladin, known to Hannah from her childhood in Clay Cross, and some more male friends, joined the girls. So drunk did they become that Hannah began walking erratically and even falling over. Two police constables noticed her behaviour but did not intervene, for which they were later criticised.

As the drink took a greater hold of Hannah she began to talk of a previous boyfriend from Clay Cross, called Walker, of whom her parents disapproved. There were rumours that she had once flung herself from the window of her home in a crude attempt at suicide when her parents forbade them to meet again. She said she was desperate to restart the relationship, whatever the cost. At the end of the evening, she was so drunk that she stayed the night with her friend Ann rather than return to her place of work.

The Rutland, behind the parish church.

The staircase in the Rutland, down which the figure of a woman 'walks' before she crosses the bar.

The next morning she returned to the Rutland Arms to take up her duties, but her filthy and dishevelled clothing shocked her workmates. However, they all went about their duties, and the Monday morning seemed to be going along as usual until Elizabeth Harding went to find Hannah, who was supposed to be in the washhouse. Her screams brought the manager running. Far from doing her chores, Hannah had wrapped a length of washing line around her neck and hanged herself from the rafters in the outside water closet. The manager cut her down but it was too late. She was dead.

Did Hannah hang herself for shame at her drunken behaviour? Or was it her continuing distress at having lost her lover, Walker, which caused her to become depressed and seek solace in alcohol? The truth will never be known. But there is no doubt that an unquiet spirit haunts the public house now known simply as 'The Rutland'.

Many a time a white figure has come down the elegant wooden staircase with 'barley sugar' spindles, to process across the bar and then leave at the far end. She was so obvious to one man that for a moment he mistook her for his daughter. The white dress could be the un-dyed work clothes of Hannah, the former employee. Is it she who 'supervises' over the cleaning being done by Jane Randall, the manageress, in the upstairs rooms? She feels a presence watching her as she goes about her chores. So strong is the feeling that she often feels bound to turn round, just in case someone is really there.

When the Randall's moved in to The Rutland, they were aware that their two young children, a son and a daughter, might become disorientated if they got up in the night. So when they heard footsteps and then the flush of the toilet, Ken quickly got up to check on the children. The toilet continued to flush, but both children were sound asleep. Could it have been a nocturnal trip of the man in black who has been seen in the red brick section of the public house, once the home of the verger of the parish church? Perhaps it was the same 'man' who often sat on the end of one little boy's bed during the night. Ken and Ann had heard the story of the nocturnal' 'bed sitter' from the previous tenants, but of course had not mentioned it to the children for fear of alarming them. They were surprised, to say the least, when their own son reported the same experience as the former occupant of the room.

Other phenomena occur in this building; glasses have been seen to move horizontally from the shelves and then drop to the floor; but they do not break. In the cellar the gas switches off from time to time and, most inconvenient of all, the water to the icemaker is switched off, leaving the bar temporarily without ice.

But the Randall family seem quite unconcerned by all this, and continue to live in harmony with their ghostly visitors, whilst giving a warm welcome to their less ethereal guests.

BIBLIOGRAPHY

Anthony, Wayne, *Haunted Derbyshire and the Peak District* (Breedon Books Publishing Co., 1997)
Armitage, Jill, *Haunted Places of Derbyshire* (Countryside Books, 2005)
Bell, David, *Derbyshire Ghosts and Legends* (Countryside Books, 1993)
Bunting, Julie, *The Earls and Dukes of Devonshire* (Footprint Press Ltd, 1997)
Craven, Maxwell and Stanley, Michael, *The Derbyshire Country House* (Breedon Books Publishing Co., 1991)
Girouard, Mark, *Guide to Hardwick Hall* (National Trust, 1989)
Krawszik, Ann, *Chesterfield – Picture the Past* (Tempus Publishing Ltd, 2005)
Leonard, John, *Derbyshire Parish Churches* (Breedon Book Publishing Co., 1993)
Matthews, David, *Around Staveley*, (Sutton Publishing, 1995)
Pearson, Ray, *Ghosts In and Around Chesterfield* (Higham Press Ltd, 1984)
Pearson, Ray, *More Ghosts In and Around Chesterfield* (Higham Press Ltd, 1986)
Redfern, Roger, *Chesterfield's Remarkable Houses* (The Cottage Press, Old Brampton, 1997)
Sadler, Geoffrey, *Foul Deeds and Suspicious Deaths* (Wharncliffe Books, 2003)
Sadler, Geoffrey, *Chesterfield History and Guide* (Tempus Publishing Ltd, 2001)
Derbyshire Villages (Countryside books/Derbyshire Federation of Womens' Institutes, 2002)
The Derbyshire Village Book (Countryside Books/Derbyshire Federation of Womens' Institutes, 1991)

And many more pamphlets, books, leaflets, articles and so on absorbed over the years.

Other local titles published by The History Press

Chesterfield: Picture the Past
ANN KRAWSZIK

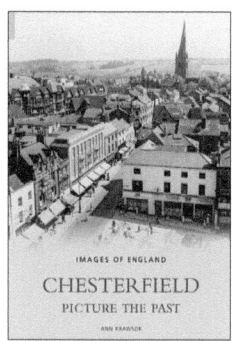

This collection of over 200 old photographs of Chesterfield is a sample of the many thousands of images which are now available to view on the award-winning website www.picturethepast.org.uk. These images, many never before published, provide a fascinating pictorial history of Chesterfield over the past 150 years. The result is a book that will delight anyone who has lived or worked in this popular market town with the leaning spire.

7524 3581 7

Buxton and the High Peak
MIKE LANGHAM, MIKE BENTLEY AND COLIN WELLS

Board's photographic business opened in the Devonshire Colonnade in the mid-1920s and when the firm closed in the 1970s its collection of glass-plate negatives was donated to the Buxton Museum for safe-keeping. This book is a second selection of images to be published from this valuable record of Buxton through the twentieth century and the choice of photographs has again been made by the local historians who compiled the first volume and who have been responsible for cataloguing the entire Board archive.

7524 3951 0

Sheffield Parks and Gardens
DOUGLAS HINDMARSH

Sheffield is justifiably proud of the parks, woodlands and open spaces which make it one of the greenest cities in Europe. However, in the early nineteenth century the town was overcrowded and polluted and there were no green spaces for leisure and recreation. This book illustrates how the parks and gardens were acquired and developed from the 1830s onwards, and shows some of the park features which have now disappeared. Also depicted are everyday events and special occasions such as Royal visits and Whitsuntide.

7524 3542 6

Belper and Milford
ADRIAN FARMER

From the eighteenth century to the present day, the cotton mill town of Belper and its smaller neighbour have reflected Britain's changing fortunes as an industrial nation – reaping the benefits of early innovations, only to lose so many of their industrial landmarks in the latter half of the twentieth century. Today the mills, along with much of both Belper and Milford, are part of the Derwent Valley Mills World Heritage Site.

7524 3376 8

If you are interested in purchasing other books published by The History Press, or in case you have difficulty finding any of our books in your local bookshop, you can also place orders directly through our website
www.thehistorypress.co.uk